PENGUIN
SPECIALS

Penguin Specials fill a gap. Written by some of today's most exciting and insightful writers, they are short enough to be read in a single sitting – when you're stuck on a train; in your lunch hour; between dinner and bedtime. Specials can provide a thought-provoking opinion, a primer to bring you up to date, or a striking piece of fiction. They are concise, original and affordable.

To browse digital and print Penguin Specials titles, please refer to **www.penguin.com.au/penguinspecials**

ALSO BY IRA NADEL

Biography: Fiction, Fact & Form

Joyce and the Jews, Culture and Texts

Various Positions, A Life of Leonard Cohen

Double Act, A Life of Tom Stoppard

A Critical Companion to Philip Roth

*Modernism's Second Act,
A Cultural Narrative*

Cathay

Ezra Pound's Orient

IRA NADEL

PENGUIN BOOKS

UK | USA | Canada | Ireland | Australia
India | New Zealand | South Africa | China

Penguin Books is part of the Penguin Random House group of companies
whose addresses can be found at global.penguinrandomhouse.com.

This paperback edition published by Penguin Group (Australia)
in association with Penguin (Beijing) Ltd, 2015

1 3 5 7 9 10 8 6 4 2

Cover design by Di Suo © Penguin Group (Australia)
Text design by Steffan Leyshon-Jones © Penguin Group (Australia)
Printed and bound in Hong Kong by Printing Express

ISBN: 9780734399533

penguin.com.cn

To Dara, Ryan and Anne

CONTENTS

Exotic Cathay

No work of Ezra Pound's, or perhaps of modernist poetry, has had the impact of *Cathay*, his collection of fourteen Chinese poems published one hundred years ago in 1915. Without any Chinese-language experience, but with a surplus of enthusiasm and gusto, Pound unleashed his widely-praised work onto the world. T.S. Eliot was an early celebrant of the thirty-two page volume, claiming that 'Pound is the inventor of Chinese poetry for our time,' while famed writers and critics including William Carlos Williams, Hilda 'H.D.' Doolittle, Marianne Moore and Gary Snyder praised the elegance, simplicity and directness of the 'translations.'[1]

For Wyndham Lewis, Pound was a transmitter 'busy with removal of old world into new quarters.' For Carl

Sandburg, 'he stains darkly and touches softly. He is . . . a biplane in the azure.'[2] By consent in *Cathay* Pound achieved 'the direct treatment of the thing' – the Imagist objective of clarity and precision – through his re-working of the Chinese texts. In *Cathay*, Pound remade his source texts in the Imagist mould embedded in the Chinese works.

In the same year as Pound's 'translations' emerged, a number of other modernist texts appeared: Gertrude Stein's *Three Lives* finally reached British shores after its initial 1909 publication in the U.S.; Amy Lowell's anthology, *Some Imagist Poets*; Ford Madox Ford's *The Good Soldier,* as well as Pound's own controversial volume *Catholic Anthology*, containing T.S. Eliot's 'The Love Song of J. Alfred Prufrock'. Virginia Woolf published her first novel, *The Voyage Out*, while D.H. Lawrence's *The Rainbow* appeared and then disappeared, suppressed almost immediately for its supposed obscenity. That same year a Leipzig newspaper printed Kafka's 'The Metamorphosis', while Joyce, Lenin and Tristan Tzara, a Dadaist artist/writer, took up residence in Zurich – a milieu later dramatised by Tom Stoppard in his play *Travesties*. However, the most memorable and outstanding poetic text of 1915 was *Cathay*, a work that presented a series of classical Chinese texts in accessible and contemporary language equal to any work being written in modern English poetry.

Cathay plays an evolutionary role in Pound's modernist project to refresh, if not re-make, the language of twentieth century poetry. The poems of Li Bai and others provided the intersection between East and West that redefined the modernist project. In a culture of poetic intensity, visual clarity and objectivity present in the poems, Pound discovered correspondences with his own program of poetic reform. What Pound did to enhance and enliven his Chinese texts was to implement his Imagist methods and principles. As a consequence, the aesthetic rather than metrical elements of his 'translations' resulted in English texts that were new and that redefined not only the place of Chinese poetry in the West but the nature of twentieth century poetry.

But what drew Pound to China, how did he write *Cathay* and why does it remain a pioneering modernist work pointing to a style and manner absorbed by others? Early twentieth century scholars, historians, translators and poets such as Herbert Giles, Laurence Binyon, Arthur Waley and W.B. Yeats will help to answer these questions and paint the picture of Pound's engagement with the Orient which strongly influenced his poetic heirs. Giles, author of *A History of Chinese Literature* (1901), initiated Pound's encounter with the Orient but the crucial figure for Pound was the American Orientalist, decorated by Emperor Meiji of Japan with the Order of the Rising Sun, Ernest Fenollosa.

Giles' *History* introduced Pound to Chinese poetry as it did for Allen Upward, Binyon and John Gould Fletcher. Professor of Chinese at the University of Cambridge and former British Consular at Ningbo, China, Giles provided the first attempt at a history of Chinese literature and one with an emphasis on translation. Giles had actually been in China from 1867–92 and had previously published *Gems of Chinese Literature* (1884).

The *History* offers a synoptic view of Chinese writing, opening with a summary of a set of Confucian classics.[3] The fifth chapter introduces the revered poet and patriot Qu Yuan, considered to be the first author of Chinese poetry to have his name associated with his work and whose suicide is remembered every year in China with the Dragon Boat Festival. His fourth century BCE school of thought, known as Chu Ci (楚辭), favoured suggestion and allusion, as well as engagement with 'wild irregular metres which consorted well with their world of irregular thoughts. Their poetry was prose run mad. It was allusive and allegorical,' Giles writes.[4] The emphasis on the wild irregular metres strongly appealed to Pound's Imagist sensibility and determination to break out of the straitjacket of English iambic pentameter.

Giles further explains that Qu Yuan 'never ends his line in deference to a prescribed number of feet, but lengthens or shortens to suit the exigency of his thought.' The idea, not the verse metric, controls the form, which is precisely what Pound was seeking in his own writing. A reader of Qu Yuan is never aware of this shift, carried away 'by [the] flow of language and rapid succession of poetical imagery'.[5] Qu Yuan's freedom with form was critical for Pound who had set out early on to restructure metre in English verse, turning first to the Greeks and then Provençal poets in an effort to have metre respond more directly to emotion. Poetry gives us 'equations for the human emotions' he wrote in *The Spirit of Romance*.[6] But neither tradition concentrated so exclusively on imagery as Chinese poetry.

In its attenuated verse forms, condensed and exact, each word in Chinese was carefully selected for its symbolic as well as immediate value. Chinese writing excelled in its use of 'concrete verbs', precise and objective word choice, to create striking and intense verse which, as Pound wrote, 'speaks at once with the vividness of painting and with the mobility of sounds.'[7] In the notebooks of the American philosopher and historian of Japanese Art, Ernest Fenollosa, and the classical Chinese poets, Pound would find the key to his poetic revolution.

From the initial publication of *Cathay*, there was fierce debate over whether the collection was translation or invention. Pound, who did not know Chinese at the time, did not let that stop him. He energetically sought to understand if not capture the poetic world of the Orient for English-language readers, determined to make that world accessible and understandable. That said, the title page of *Cathay* cites Pound as translator and indicates that he worked 'from the Chinese of Rihaku' and from the notes of Ernest Fenollosa aided by the 'decipherings' of Professors Mori and Ariga, which leaves the reader in somewhat of a quandary as to who actually wrote these poems.

The title *Cathay* likely originated with Marco Polo who called one of his books in his twelfth century *Travels* 'Cathay' to designate a remote northwestern region of China. Pound, who owned a multi-volume edition of Polo's works, would have recalled the term and its importance as an early idea of the country. The anglicised version of *Catai*, Cathay originated from the nomadic people who founded the Liao Dynasty which ruled northern China from 907–1125. The term later became an abstract expression of European and American views of China long before Ernest Fenollosa's research into its literature and culture. For explorers in the sixteenth century, Cathay represented a fabled if not visionary home of the earthly paradise or Middle Kingdom represented by the Tang and Song dynasties (618–690 and 705–907; 960–1279), with the Emperor often referred to as the 'Son of Heaven'. The work of Confucius also extended this idea of Cathay. China, at the supposed centre of the world, was also considered to be the centre of civilisation.[8]

However, ambiguity existed as there was no clarity concerning whether 'Catai' referred to China or to another portion of the country. But Cathay was not a country separate from China as many in the seventeenth century, relying on misconstrued travellers' reports, originally believed.

Cathay's repeated identification with, and even perception as, China sustained an element of the visionary associated, at least in western minds, with the semi-mythic, exotic and adventurous. Searching for a passage to Cathay was a long sought for goal of Europeans beginning with Columbus, as well as Portuguese and Spanish explorers throughout the sixteenth century. Even the French explorer Champlain sought a route to China as one of the great objects of his trip across the Atlantic to what became Canada.[9]

Tales of imagined, literary voyagers to Cathay found early expression in the work of François Rabelais. In the fourth Book of *Gargantua and Pantagruel* (1548), Pantagruel's fleet heads off to the East on a trip to take them 'near Cathay in Upper India'. Geography here meant very little. Another literary traveller to Cathay was John Milton, although he reflected confusion over the actual designation of Cathay versus China. In the eleventh book of *Paradise Lost* (2nd ed., 1674), he still viewed

Cathay as distinct from China. In addition, Voltaire speaks of China in his *Lettres Philosophiques* (1733) and in 1755 wrote a play *L'Orphelin de la Chine* (*The Orphan of China*) and incorporated China in various guises in his work. He opens his *Essay on Universal History: The Manners and Spirit of Nations* (1756) with China, admiring its technology, governance and Confucianism. And his '*Catéchisme chinois*' ('Chinese Catechism') appears in his *Philosophical Dictionary* (1764). His sources for many of these ideas: Jesuit letters and writings.

Byron refers to Cathay in *Don Juan* XII.ix.9, while Tennyson condescendingly includes it in the concluding section of 'Locksley Hall' when he writes: 'Better fifty years of Europe than a cycle of Cathay.' Ralph W. Emerson and Whitman further promoted the idea of Cathay in the nineteenth century and may have indirectly influenced Pound's decision to title the book, although Emerson's interests were broadly Asian, not exclusively Chinese. Other American writers, including Oliver Wendell Holmes, refer to Cathay in their work. In the early twentieth century, scholars used 'Cathay' as a shorthanded way of expressing the mystery of China, a world of contemplation, poise, artistic excellence, exoticism and refinement wrapped around by ancient history and civil order. The composite narrative of China meant thousands of years of successive civilisations without such European upheavals as the French Revolution, the

Revolutions of 1848 or the Russian Revolution of 1917. All of these references suggest a remoteness as well as familiarity summarised at the end of Hart Crane's poem *The Bridge* (1930) when the American poet simply asks, seeking the meaning of what Columbus discovered, 'Is it Cathay?'

In China, nation and culture were perceived to be one, a union immensely attractive to writers like Pound who perceived Confucian balance and social practice at work. Embodying this fascination with the Orient at the outset of the twentieth century was W. A. P. Martin's *The Lore of Cathay or the Intellect of China* (1901). Martin was a distinguished China scholar and for several years President of the Foreign University of Beijing. But it is Pound who emerges as the first major twentieth century poet to incorporate ideas of China into a major cycle of global poetry and project them into European and American culture at large, fulfilling Whitman's declaration of 1860, 'at last the Orient comes.'[10]

I

Pound and the Invention of China

'Japan I am sometimes interested in,
but China is the magical place'
Marianne Moore, 1932

But why China? Surprisingly the answer is, in part, Philadelphia. The connections between Philadelphia and the Orient ran deep, and not only because Beijing and Philadelphia share the same latitude. Several entrepreneurs tried to grow silkworms and Chinese tea to capitalise on the geographic connection between Philadelphia and China but, of course, climate interfered and the projects failed. As early as 1828, a giant pagoda, locally known as 'the Temple of Confucius', was built in Fairmont Park and a merchant named Nathan Dunn amassed a collection of 1200 objects from his time in China and opened a museum in 1839; another museum, based on the collection of a John Peters, opened in 1847 and was still operating during Pound's time in the city. In a further link to the East, in 1897, a Philadelphia lawyer, John Luther Long, published a novel, *Madame Butterfly*. It was adapted into a play in 1900 and in 1904 became a successful opera by Puccini. Pound, interested in music, may have heard it. [11]

Closer to home, Pound's parents owned an eighteenth century screen book of Chinese paintings and ideograms which Pound often studied. Its provenance is unclear but it likely originated with his mother's grandfather, Hiram Parker, who sailed for a time to the Orient. Its importance, however, is undisputed. The sequence of Oriental scenes with its accompanying poems in Chinese and Japanese ideograms became instrumental when Pound acquired it in 1928, turning it into his sourcebook for the 'Seven Lakes Canto' (Canto 49). The fourteen fold volume consisted of eight ink paintings, eight poems in Chinese and eight poems in Japanese, remained with Pound until his death.

At the time, the Philadelphia Museum of Art also had an expanding Asian collection, capitalising on Oriental furniture, ceramics, lacquerware and other decorative arts from the Chinese, Japanese and Indian exhibitors at the 1876 Philadelphia Centennial Exhibition. The images of China depicted in the paintings, porcelains, silks and lacquer plates recreated a mythical, mysterious and distant world that was focused, precise, objective and elegant in detail and in harmony with nature. Such visual exposure prepared Pound for a more detailed study of the art when he arrived in London in August 1908. The materiality of Chinese culture in its Philadelphia context not only primed Pound for its later acceptance via lectures, study and reading but affected his overall sympathy and curiosity towards the Orient.

The young poet-to-be was also heir to an American Orientalism emanating from the transcendentalists of New England with Confucius at the centre. Emerson drew sporadically on Chinese materials in his journals and essays and attempted to translate portions of the Confucian Four Books into English. He also read travel books and diplomatic papers dealing with the East. His theory of natural language incorporated elements of Chinese ideograms and the symbolic, visual language of Chinese. 'Words are signs of natural facts,' he wrote in his essay 'Nature'.[12] Ironically, at the end of the nineteenth century, Ernest Fenollosa began to teach the works of Emerson to several of his advanced students in Japan and combine readings of Emerson with the study of classic Chinese poems. Fenollosa's the 'Chinese Written Character', not surprisingly, embraces Emerson's ideas about language and poetry uniting Western and Eastern concepts.[13] Chinese for Pound partly meant the recovery or reinvention of the innocent speech of Adam, returning to a world that Emerson idealised.[14]

Henry David Thoreau similarly explored China and found the Orient to be a sympathetic and stimulating intellectual space. Thoreau published excerpts from the Confucian Four Books in *The Dial* and cites him several times in *Walden*. A passage from the *Analects* 8:13 appears in his 'Resistance to Civil Government'. Thoreau also anticipated Pound in his celebration of the 'Make it New' values found in Confucianism. In *Walden*, he cites the engraved motto on the bathtub of King Tching Thang which he paraphrases as 'renew thyself completely each day', adding that 'morning brings back the heroic ages'. In *A Week on the Concord and Merrimack Rivers*, Thoreau asks his readers to stop reading and enter the phenomenal world, the 'unexplored Pacific Ocean of futurity' that reaches to the shores of China.[15] Pound, as one critic noted, continued a New England tradition of Oriental awareness although his focus was on the aesthetic not the religious dimension of the culture.[16]

Pound was also aware of a tradition of American travellers to the Orient, not only Commander Perry, who first visited Japan in 1853, but Henry Adams who travelled there with the artist John La Farge in 1886. Gertrude Stein visited Japan with her brother in 1892, and Harriet Monroe visited China in 1910–11, returning to Chicago to found *Poetry* magazine, an important outlet for Pound who became its foreign editor.

Japan and China constantly competed, but on 10 January 1917, Pound himself declared to the lawyer/patron John Quinn in New York that 'China is fundamental, Japan is not.'[17]

Familial ties among the Pounds maintained an actual China connection. In the autumn of 1913, the Inspector General of Mints in the new Republic of China, Far-san T. Sung visited Homer Pound, Ezra's father, at the U.S. Mint where he worked. He suggested Homer Pound join him in the new China. In response to his father possibly being offered a post in China, the son writes 'China is interesting. VERY. Make sure which Chinese government is giving you the job and then blaze away.' The letter ends with 'send on your Chinamen as soon as you like' regarding a visit by Sung. When Sung did meet Pound in London in the winter of 1914, he was optimistic about finding Pound, himself, a job in Peking. Encouraged, Pound wrote to his father that Sung seems fairly sure of 'fixing you in Pekin and optimistic about yours truly. We may yet be a united family.'[18] Nothing came of it, however.

Pound and China in London

Pound, who arrived in London ostensibly to meet Yeats, continued his education on Oriental matters with the activist/lawyer/writer Allen Upward, who directed

Pound to the Chinese classics. Pound had left the United States in the early summer of 1908 for Venice where he published his first book *A Lume Spento* at his own expense that July. By late August, he headed to London and under the guidance of the generous and welcoming British novelist May Sinclair was introduced to Ford Madox Ford, editor of the *English Review* and soon to be the first to publish Pound in England. Pound would also encounter Henry James and Wyndham Lewis.[19] But Upward became his immediate Oriental connection. Like Upward, Pound published in *The New Age* magazine and was as outspoken about political and literary matters as the Englishman. In 1913, a series of Upward's poems, 'Scented Leaves from a Chinese Jar', appeared in *Poetry* magazine, forwarded to Harriet Monroe by Pound who later included nine of the poems in his anthology *Des Imagistes*.

By October 1913, Upward had Pound reading Confucius and Mencius in French, notably M.G. Pauthier's 1841 volume *Doctrine de Confucius ou Les Quatre Livres de philosophie morale et politique de la Chine* containing the *Analects* (2 vols.), the *Great Digest* and *The Unwobbling Pivot*. Pound would later translate the last two and condense a good deal of Confucian thought in Canto 13. The first sentence of the Introduction of Pauthier, entitled 'Civilisation Chinoise', reads *'la civilisation chinoise est sans aucun doute la plus ancienne civilisation du monde existante'* ('the Chinese civilisation is without a doubt the most ancient civilisation existing in the world') followed by a claim that China possesses *'une grande culture morale qu'il serait difficile de surpasser, même de nos jours'* ('a grand moral culture which will be difficult to surpass even in our time').[20] Upward likely also showed Pound his translation *Sayings of Confucius* (1904) which appeared in his 'Wisdom of the East' series. Importantly, Upward saw Confucius not as a literary figure but a leader with administrative savvy. He was a practical statesman who also valued culture, the perfect mix for Pound. And not only did Confucius lead an exemplary life but he possessed a literary sensibility, editing the classic anthology of ancient Chinese poetry.

In London, the British Museum quickly supplanted Upward, becoming Pound's laboratory where he broadened his education in Oriental art and Confucian ideals. By 1909 he became a regular visitor to the British Museum, eager to see its collections of Chinese paintings and illustrated publications, often publicised through the illustrated talks of Laurence Binyon, then an Assistant Keeper in the Department of Prints and Drawings. Pound met Binyon – dramatist, art historian and poet, who had won the prestigious Newdigate poetry prize at Oxford in 1891 – through Elkin Mathews, Pound and Binyon's publisher.

Pound attended Binyon's illustrated lecture on Oriental and European Art given at the Royal Albert Hall, on 15 March 1909. One of Binyon's key points was the analogies between the literary and artistic developments in China and Europe. Promoted by Japan's Ashikaga Shoguns, a dynasty of the Ashikaga family that governed as military rulers over Japan from roughly 1336–1573, the arts flourished. Pound saw an immediate parallel with the fifteenth century Italian Renaissance in Florence and figures like the *condottiero* (warlord) Sigismondo Malatesta, celebrated as a leader *and* patron of the arts, who would appear early in *The Cantos*, Pound's epic-length poem including history drawn from Renaissance Italy, China and America.

The content of Binyon's series, advertised as 'Art & Thought in East & West: Parallels and Contrasts,' was a blend of ideas from Okakura Kakuzō's influential *The Ideals of the East*, reviewed by Binyon in the *Times Literary Supplement*, as well as from his own *Paintings in the Far East* (1908), a valuable outline of Oriental art. In addition, in 1909, Binyon published *Japanese Art*, which was succeeded in 1911 by *Flight of the Dragon* on Oriental aesthetics. By November 1912, Binyon's scholarship and acumen led to his appointment as director of the new sub-department at the museum to house its Chinese and Japanese paintings and prints.

Pound had actually visited the British Museum

Prints and Drawings Students' Room, which housed the Oriental collection, twice before his first meeting with Binyon and attendance at the Albert Hall lectures. Located in the long space between the Prints and Drawings Gallery and the Asiatic Saloon, it was where students could examine first-hand recent museum acquisitions in a studious environment. It was there that Binyon, seated at a desk in the open-plan area, daily oversaw visitors who had to present credentials and an admission ticket and sign in. The register records visits by art critics like Roger Fry, Clive Bell and the Japanese art historian Hogitaro Inada, as well as such artists as Lawrence Alma-Tadema, Edmund Dulac, Lucien Pissarro, Walter Sickert and Duncan Grant. Pound, Yeats and the young war poet Isaac Rosenberg were among the poets who appeared, Pound visiting as early as February 1909. At the time, the Prints and Drawings Room was 'the most exciting division of the British Museum in terms of acquisitions.'[21]

At his desk Binyon often sorted the horde of new objects ranging from handscrolls to painted panels, canvases, works on silk and woodblock impressions known as *nishiki-e* or brocade prints. Most of them were associated with the *ukiyo-e* or 'floating world' movement of urban Edo, modern day Tokyo.[22] Binyon took notes on all of these items for a comprehensive catalogue that he would complete in 1916. Binyon and the visits to the august Prints and Drawings room by Pound left a lasting impression on the young poet recalled in Cantos 80 and 87. In Canto 87 Pound honours Binyon and the Oriental aesthetic of gradualness, a sense of increasing if measured intensity progressively experienced: '"BinBin" is beauty./ Slowness is beauty.'

To highlight Oriental art, between June 1910 and April 1912, the British Museum held a comprehensive 'Exhibition of Chinese and Japanese Paintings' housed in the museum's newly-constructed White Wing. An earlier exhibition with a similar title was held in the Prints and Drawings Gallery in 1888, although only thirteen of the approximately 237 exhibits were of Chinese origin. In the 1910–12 exhibition, there were 108 Chinese paintings and 126 Japanese paintings reflecting the persistent interest in aesthetic sources for the fashionable *Japonisme* and *Chinoiserie* of the time – plus an aesthetic attraction to the colour, precision, unity, imagery and techniques of Oriental art.

The exhibit gave the public their first chance to review a large collection of Chinese and Japanese works, Binyon wrote the guide to the show. [23] The works, and Binyon's commentaries, stressed the originality of the art plus its links to the West, especially his favoured 'The Admonitions of the Instructress to Court Ladies' acquired by the museum in 1903 and item No. 1 in the Guide. This Chinese narrative painted handscroll on silk, with its artistic jade toggle and nine of the original twelve painted scenes, became a feature of the exhibition.

The items in the show reinforced a concept of behaviour and social decorum similar to that of the West. In the first week of 1913, Pound told Dorothy in a letter that he had spent the day in searches at the British Museum and that 'I contemplated mediaeval Japanese prints at the B.M. and feel ages older and wiser.'[24]

Two further exhibits in 1913 extended Pound's awareness of Oriental art. The first was held at the Victoria and Albert Museum, a loan exhibit of principally R.H. Benson's collection of early Chinese pottery of the Tang and Ming dynasties. The V&A used the exhibit to publicise a series of new display halls designed to house an even larger collection of Chinese porcelain, bronzes, textiles and furniture. In one of those rooms, Pound likely saw a dragon-emblazoned imperial robe of pale green satin. A month later in *Poetry*, Pound published a short poem with reference to 'a green coat out of China/ With dragons worked upon it.' He wrote this Chinese-influenced and inspired verse before he received any of the Fenollosa material.

The second show was at the Whitechapel Gallery where an earlier exhibit in 1901 on Chinese art drew more than 135000 visitors. The 1913 Whitechapel exhibition included five lectures on Chinese history, painting, pottery and metalwork. The exhibit opened in October but Pound likely had an advance viewing because he knew the chair: Laurence Binyon. Throughout 1912 Binyon had helped Fenollosa's widow organise, edit and illustrate her husband's notes on sculpture and painting resulting in *Epochs of Chinese and Japanese Art*. Binyon likely facilitated the meeting between Mrs Fenollosa and Pound. He may have also suggested a visit to the exhibition to Pound to prepare for the encounter.

Meanwhile, the collection of Oriental prints at the British Museum soon grew too large for its original accommodation and was moved in late 1914 to a newly expanded north wing. But frustrated with the closure of the original print room, Pound found a new centre at the V & A. There, a new loan exhibition of Japanese Colour Prints was to open which would include seven prints by Ando Hiroshige who would influence John Gould Fletcher, another member of Pound's growing Imagist school of poetry. One masterwork to be shown was a rare triptych, 'Mountain River on the Kiso Road'. This was part of the *ukiyo-e* prints, also known as 'floating world' prints, intricate woodblock prints popular of the late eighteenth and nineteenth centuries. Pound's progress was proceeding slowly from Japanese art to Chinese poetry.

Parallel to this was Pound's increasingly serious study of Confucius, encouraged by Upward. In the Chinese philosopher, Pound found a figure whose principles of cultural advancement and political rule balanced his own artistic sensibility. He quickly became a model for the young American poet who by October 1913 could tell Dorothy Shakespear, his future wife, that he was immersed in the thought and life of the Chinese figure.[25]

His forthcoming meeting with the widow of Ernest Fenollosa would accelerate the pace of his involvement with the Orient initiated by Philadelphia, Binyon, Upward and soon Arthur Waley, a widely respected translator of Japanese literature.

Pound saw China before he read it, preparing him for his later reworking of Fenollosa's Chinese poems, the editing of various Noh plays (traditional plays of Japan known for their clarity of language and move-ment and soon to influence both Pound and Yeats) organised by Fenollosa, and revising Fenollosa's essays on Chinese writing. He was also closely reading Fenollosa's two-volume *Epochs of Chinese and Japanese Art*, the posthumously published survey of Chinese and Japanese art edited from notes by his wife. In some ways, the book became a model for what Pound would do with *Cathay* in terms of incorporating the work of other scholars into a new, single text.

Pound's visual curiosity with China and initial study of its literature preceded his meeting with Mrs Mary Fenollosa. The first of four meetings between the two occurred at the home of the Indian nationalist poet Sarojini Naidu, on 29 September 1913.[26] Pound knew Naidu through Tagore, whom Pound met the previous year. Pound had edited and wrote an introduction to six of Tagore's poems which appeared in the December 1912 issue of *Poetry*. It is possible that Mary Fenollosa had read Pound's lengthy essay on Tagore in the *Fortnightly Review* of March 1913, the same month his 'A Few Don'ts by an Imagiste' appeared in *Poetry*. She also likely read some of his poetry before they met. After their first meeting, he sent her some additional work including several poems that appeared in the April 1913 issue of *Poetry*.

Originally from Mobile, Alabama, Mary McNeill (later Fenollosa) was both married and, unfortunately, widowed young, her husband died just two years after they wed. Hearing of her loss, an earlier suitor wrote to her from Japan with an offer of marriage. She sailed in 1890 with an infant son and remarried, but two years later divorced her new husband and returned to Mobile now with a second child. Her exposure to Japan began a long love affair with Japanese culture and art.

In 1895 she learned about a job in the Asian art division of the Boston Museum of Fine Arts. She applied, was hired and began to work for Ernest Fenollosa. They quickly fell in love and Fenollosa divorced his wife to marry Mary. The scandal forced them to move to New

York and then to Japan, in 1897, where he took up a professorship. There, they quickly became the centre of a group of Japanese and American artists and writers.

While her husband researched Japanese art and culture, advised American collectors such as Charles Freer, and purchased items for the Asian collection of the Boston Museum, Mary Fenollosa began to write poetry and fiction. Her first novel, published under the name of Sidney McCall, appeared in 1901, the same year as her article 'Hiroshige, the Artist of Mist, Snow and Rain'. Her next two novels, *The Breath of the Gods* and *The Dragon Painter* were both set in Japan, the first appearing under her own name. It was adapted as a Broadway play, film and opera. The second, under the name of Sidney McCall, tells the story of an aging Japanese artist who fears the introduction of Western ways in his homeland and seeks to pass on his traditional practices to a younger generation. It later became a film.

Mary Fenollosa published six more novels and a book of children's verses, *Blossoms from a Japanese Garden*. She continued to publish through 1918, living on until 1954. Importantly, Mary Fenollosa's knowledge of the Orient was direct and immediate: indeed, when completing her husband's unfinished *Epochs of Chinese and Japanese Art* – Fenollosa died unexpectedly in London in 1908 on the eve of his return to America – she revisited Japan to check dates and other facts and wrote the foreword to the volume which appeared in 1912. Mary Fenollosa was one of the first Americans Pound met who had actually lived in Japan and absorbed its culture.

In a late interview, Pound recalled that he had originally been dissatisfied with the translations of Chinese poetry he had read in Giles' *History a*nd wanted to 'get some Chinese'. He then met Mrs Fenollosa and learned that 'Fenollosa had been scrapping with academic fatheads and he'd left his manuscript with her and she sat on it.'[27] The timing for Pound was perfect.

The conversation at their first meeting, according Zhaoming Qian, focused on Chinese art and Fenollosa's efforts at assembling the Freer collection of Asian art in Washington, D.C. Mary Fenollosa may have also mentioned her husband's enthusiasm for Chinese classical poetry which likely excited Pound. In the next day or so, Pound went to the Isle of Wight to visit his tutor in Chinese literature, Allen Upward, to share his enthusiasm at meeting Fenollosa's widow. Upward encouraged Pound to continue reading Giles' *History*, in addition to Pauthier's *Les quatre liveres de philosophie morale et politique de la Chine*. He may have also read Giles' *Chinese Poetry in English Verse* (1898). Upward by this time had published several translations from the Confucian *Analects* in the *New Freewoman*.

By 2 October 1913, Pound could not resist telling

Dorothy Shakespear that he 'seems to be getting orient from all quarters.' He had been stocking up on Confucius and Mencius: 'I suppose they'll keep me calm for a week or so.'[28] He had also viewed real Japanese prints at Harriet Shaw Weaver's home – not reproductions. As he would enthusiastically write in his series 'Affirmations', 'China is no less stimulating than Greece . . . these new masses of unexplored arts and facts are pouring in to the vortex of London. They cannot help bringing about changes as great as the Renaissance.'[29] At this time, Pound also produced four Chinese poems adapted from H.A. Giles. In these and *Cathay*, he benefited equally from his encounter with Chinese art and Fenollosa's scholarship.

The second meeting of Pound and Mary Fenollosa took place at the elegant Café Royal on 6 October 1913. Sarojini Naidu and William Heinemann, the publisher who brought out Fenollosa's posthumous *Epochs of Chinese and Japanese Art* (1912), also attended. Mrs Fenollosa used the occasion to narrate her husband's work on Chinese poetry. Pound had already skimmed Pauthier's French translation of Confucius and the early chapters of Giles' *History*, so he was able to comment on some of the merits of Oriental poetry. In a letter to Dorothy the next day, Pound celebrated the Chinese inability to create a long poem: 'They hold if a man can't say what he wants to in 12 lines, he'd better leave it unsaid.'[30] This condensation was what Pound especially respected in Chinese poetry and what his Imagist agenda sought to establish. In contradicting the rhetoric, diction and elaborateness of Georgian poetry, and the allusiveness of Symbolist writing, both of which succeeded the Victorians, Pound sought to 'cut direct' as he wrote in his study of the sculptor Gaudier-Brezska. Chinese poetry showed him not only the way but that it could be done.

The third meeting between Pound and Mrs Fenollosa was on 11 October and involved two plays and dinner with Heinemann. But most interestingly, the personality as well as textual practice of Mary Fenollosa appears to have matched Pound's. She was assertive, definite, unswayed and exact. In her foreword for the second edition of *Epochs of Chinese and Japanese Art*, she noted the addition of previous omissions, as well as her absolute rejection, suggested by an academic advisor, to abolish 'all Japanese pronunciation of the old Chinese names, replacing them by the Chinese now in use.' She personally and vehemently opposed 'so drastic' a change as Pound would later object to alterations in his own long work, *The Cantos*.[31]

The tone of her writing echoes that of her husband (and of Pound) who at the end of the introduction to *Epochs*, assembled by Mrs Fenollosa, expresses ideas Pound supported and later expanded:

> Chronology alone is not the key to classification. It is,
> of course, the inner flow of real causes that we follow
> . . . [but] it is not names but powers that we deal with.
> Our plan is to take the most creative and dominant
> work of a period and describe it as the chief affair.[32]

Through her meetings with Pound, Mary Fenollosa sensed an aesthetic and concept of poetry similar not only to her husband's but to her own.

A few weeks after their third meeting, Mary Fenollosa summoned Pound to her hotel in Trafalgar Square. Morley's Hotel, founded in 1832, occupied an entire block front to the east of Trafalgar Square at the entrance to The Strand. There, in an oracular and prophetic-like tone, emphasising both her dedication to her husband's work and her own authority, she announced that he, Pound, was the *only* person who could finish the work on Chinese poetry, Noh, and his prose the way her husband would have wanted. She then departed for America and soon after sent him the manuscript materials.[33]

Fenollosa and the Source Material

Ernest Fenollosa, the Harvard-educated art historian and political economist from Salem, Massachusetts, first went to Tokyo in 1878. There, at the tender age of twenty-five, he began to study traditional Japanese art and initiated a movement to preserve its best forms. He also began to study Noh drama and by 1885 recommended the re-introduction of purely Japanese art techniques into schools.

At the time, the Japanese did not regard the images and objects in their temples as works of art. The Japanese also believed their own artistic traditions were inferior to those of the West. From 1876–1878, the Italian artist Antonio Fontanesi was invited to Tokyo to teach European oil painting techniques – more precisely Renaissance perspective, shadowing, anatomy and modelling – in an effort to imitate Western traditions. Two other Italians joined him as foreign advisors to the new Technical Fine Arts School, the first government art school in Japan. Fenollosa opposed this imposition, lecturing in 1882 to a group of influential Japanese that Japanese art was superior to western art which 'describes any object at hand mechanically, forgetting the most import point, expression of Idea'.[34]

By 1886 Fenollosa was appointed commissioner of fine arts for registering all art treasures of Japan and responsible for teaching Japanese artistic techniques in schools. In 1890, however, he accepted the positon of Curator of Oriental Art at the Boston Museum of Fine Arts. Seven years later he returned to Japan with his new wife Mary. He would later continue to lecture and write in the U.S. and England. He was considered the leading Orientalist of his time.

Pound's initial interest in Fenollosa may have been an attraction to his adventurousness and achievements. At the opening of his introduction to his *Noh or Accomplishment*, Pound writes that 'the life of Ernest Fenollosa was the romance par excellence of modern scholarship. He went to Japan as a professor of economics. He ended as Imperial Commissioner of Arts.'[35] It may be an exaggeration, Pound continues, 'to say that he had saved Japanese art for Japan' but Fenollosa singularly re-established the pre-eminence of Japanese art for the Japanese. To Pound he was heroic, a quality he also ascribed to Malatesta, Confucius, Thomas Jefferson and Mussolini.

Fenollosa's initial purpose in arriving at Yokohama in 1878 was to teach philosophy but he soon became a passionate student and advocate of East Asian art, making him a celebrity in Japan. Some have credited him with restoring the brush over the Western pencil in Japanese elementary schools. When he became Imperial Commissioner of Fine Arts in the Ministry of Culture in 1886, Fenollosa launched a country-wide effort to create an official catalogue of Japanese art and architecture and during the process discovered a set of ancient Chinese scrolls brought to Japan by travelling monks, furthering his interest in exploring connections between Japanese and Chinese art. The idea of listing art works as national treasures was a Western practice unheard of until then in Japan. The contemporary Japanese philosopher and critic Kojin Karatani declared 'it was Fenollosa who invented Japanese art.'[36] When Fenollosa died in England in 1908, the Japanese sent a warship for his ashes to return him to Japan for burial near Kyoto.

By mid-December 1913, Pound was immersed in the Fenollosa material then sent to him from America by Mary Fenollosa. At that time he wrote to William Carlos Williams from Stone Cottage, which he shared with Yeats as they explored Noh drama, that he is 'placid and happy and busy. Dorothy is learning Chinese. I've all old Fenollosa's treasures in manuscript.'[37] The treasures consisted of notebooks that recorded five years of Fenollosa's study of Chinese poetry in Japan, including two years of intensive work, between 1899–1901, with Professor Mori, a Japanese literary scholar who practised *kanshi*, the art of writing poems in Classical Chinese.[38] Mori, however, did not speak English, so Fenollosa brought with him his former philosophy student Nagai Ariga who assisted with translating Mori's Japanese. For two years the three worked through 'Rihaku' (the Japanese name for the Chinese poet Li Bai, also known as Li Po), two large notebooks containing glosses, cribs, comments and scholarly apparatus for 64 poems which form the backbone of *Cathay*.

Fenollosa also encouraged Mori to provide a set of lectures on Chinese literary history beginning with the inventions of the written characters. A Mr Hirata interpreted and the talks filled three notebooks. The original *Cathay* contained selections from some 150 notebooks in *vers libre* ('free verse') translations drawn from Fenollosa's detailed notes on the Chinese texts. Fenollosa offered almost exact, literal renderings of the original Chinese poems that resulted in awkward English.

But when Pound sat down with the Fenollosa notes dealing with poetry – compiled like the other material in Tokyo – what did he find? Chinese characters for the original poems followed interlinearly by their Japanese pronunciations and rough translations. More precisely, Fenollosa, according to Humphrey Carpenter, a Pound biographer, first copied down the original Chinese characters, then wrote out phonetic transcriptions using the Japanese pronunciations and records of his assistants in Tokyo. He then made a character-by-character translation into English and finally provided a line-by-line rendering with interpretative notes when necessary.[39]

Pound first began working with the more 'polished' Noh plays after receiving the Fenollosa materials; it was not until November 1914 that he turned his attention to the Chinese poetry notebooks. The Noh, however, offered an entryway and he began to review the materials at Stone Cottage where he had gone to spend the winter assisting Yeats. Both soon found the texts fascinating, Fenollosa writing that in the Noh plays 'we see great characters operating under the conditions of spirit-life' which made them 'a storehouse of history, and a great moral force for the whole social order.'[40] This had tremendous appeal to Yeats who tried to link Noh with Irish folk literature and who would write the introduction to *Certain Noble Plays of Japan* (1916).

For Pound, Noh demonstrated a certain unity of image through minimalist language and setting which corresponded to his Imagist ideals reinforced by Chinese verse. The parallel with Chinese poetry was explicit, the technique similar as Pound began to fulfil Mary Fenollosa's admonition to edit a book on Noh drama and an anthology of Chinese poetry.

Prior to delving into Fenollosa's notes on Chinese poetry, Pound had already discovered an early Oriental example for his Imagist technique to equal his identification of suggestion he had earlier recognized in Provençal and Tuscan poetry. This was a feature of Qu Yuan's poetry – but more importantly, Qu Yuan (sometimes Romanised as Ch'u Yuan) reinforced Pound's own Imagist aesthetic as outlined in Giles. The American poet understood the impact of classical Chinese poets. Pound would soon incorporate the vivid phrases and objective approach of Qu Yuan when re-making Fenollosa's transcriptions of Chinese poetry for *Cathay*.

Four of the six lyrics that make up Pound's contribution to the first Imagist anthology, *Des Imagistes* (1914), with its eleven contributors (including Joyce, H.D., Amy Lowell and William Carlos Williams) and edited by Pound, were modelled on Chinese poems previously rendered by Giles: 'After Ch'u Yuan', 'Liu Ch'e', 'Fan-Piece for Her Imperial Lord' and 'Ts'ai Chi'h'. Preceding Pound's Chinese poems in the anthology were 'Δ᾽ΩΡΙΑ' and 'The Return'. Pound's imagist contributions, drawing on their Chinese sources, are succinct and precise. 'Ts'ai Chi'h' reads:

> The petals fall in the fountain,
>   the orange coloured rose-leaves,
> Their ochre clings to the stone.

'Fan-Piece for Her Imperial Lord' is similarly exact:

> O fan of white silk,
>   clear as frost on the grass-blade,
> You also are laid aside.

This melancholic haiku-styled poem by Pound is a redaction of a ten-line version found in Giles focusing on the fate of the imperial concubine Lady Ban who refused to ride with the Emperor in his palanquin. The purity of style and syntax suggests a disengaged almost mandarin (objective, unemotional but eloquent) quality that is also specific.

The four poems display a growing sense of concentration in Pound's poetry where the pictorial power of imagery dominates, a feature learned from Qu Yuan. Pound reprinted the four Chinese poems in his collection *Lustra* (1917). Importantly, Pound was primed to create Chinese poetry and was doing so before he immersed himself in the Fenollosa materials.

Japan, the Orient and Imagism

Japan became an important part of Pound's Oriental outlook but, as with Chinese, he could not understand the language. His sources for grasping it were varied, ranging from T.E. Hulme's Poets' Club, where discussions of Haiku took place, to debates with the Imagist F.S. Flint who imitated the style of Japanese verse and published an important essay on Japanese poetry.[41] At the Poets' Club, as F.S. Flint recalled, 'we proposed at various times to replace [traditional English poetry] by pure *vers libre*, by the Japanese *tanka* and *haikai*; we all wrote dozens of the latter as an amusement.'[42] The Imagists, initially attempting to imitate the French Symbolists, soon found themselves pulled to Oriental poetry. The idea that Japanese *visual aesthetics* could be just as important to avant-garde poetry in the West as

Japanese *verse conventions* was compelling. But this first occurred to Richard Aldington, not Pound.

Aldington derived 'The River', appearing in the *Des Imagiste* anthology edited by Pound, directly from two Japanese colour prints in the British Museum Print Room.[43] The incorporation of several poems by T.E. Hulme in Pound's *Riposte* (1912) also acknowledges the visual tradition of Japanese poetry because of their treatment of image and style. During this period there was also new recognition of Japan not as a picturesque backwater but as a forward-looking society ever since the defeat of Russia in 1905 in Manchuria. To mark their new international prominence, the Japanese government sponsored a magnificent exhibitions of Japanese architecture, visual art and landscape gardening in London in 1910. More than eight million visitors attended, including Ford Madox Ford who went twice.

Importantly, at this time there was little direct knowledge of China in Europe, partly because of the dominance of Japan. Due to its industrial and military power, supported by magnificent exhibitions of Japanese culture, Edwardian England perceived Japan as a centre of modernity. Japan was also reaching out to the West, accepting military advice from France, industrial advice from England, agricultural advice from the U.S. and legal and medical advice from Germany. China was not and possessed only a distinguished past but, seemingly, no future. Binyon, in fact, wrote that 'the Japanese look to China' as only a 'classic land'.[44] Consequently, ideas and even images of China in the West were constructed rather than informed; distortions like the prevalence of the 'Yellow Peril' persisted. There was a general ignorance of even the chronology, as well as the aesthetics, of China and Chinese art which forced Pound back to the more accessible details of Japan often rendered in Japanese woodblock prints when visualising the East.

Drama also had a role. Pound's *Noh or Accomplishment* (1917) reprints the four plays from *Certain Noble Plays of Japan* along with a new introduction by Pound to replace the one Yeats provided in 1916.[45] The critical response to Noh, however, was not as positive as Pound had hoped. Although it was his passion from 1913 to 1916, he treated the work as a re-creation rather than a translation, similar to *Cathay*. Critics, however, understood the two volumes of 1916 and 1917 not as original works, but translations and no more. In 1915, Pound did attempt his own original Noh but abandoned it. In his introduction to the second volume of *Noh or Accomplishment*, Pound explained that 'the art of allusion . . . is at the root of the Noh' and that it is the 'art of splendid posture, of dancing and chanting, and of acting that is not mimetic.'[46]

Pound's interest in Japanese Noh and Japanese writing did not derive only from Fenollosa. Gordon Craig's journal *The Mask* (1908–29) regularly featured discussions of Japanese theatre and its artistic principles. In 1911, Pound read *The Flight of the Dragon* by Binyon which dealt with the theory and practice of art in China and Japan. That summer Pound was also in correspondence with Yonejiro Noguchi who would lecture at Oxford on Japanese Poetry. Noguchi published 'What is a Hokku Poem?' in *Rhythm* in January 1913; his Oxford lectures would appear as *The Spirit of Japanese Poetry*. He visited Pound and Yeats at Stone Cottage in 1913. Noguchi also dined with Pound in London, and later Pound told his parents that Japanese writing was 'interesting litterateur of the second order'. But the 'acquaintance may grow and there's no telling when one will want to go to Japan'.[47]

Pound also likely read B.H. Chamberlain on Japanese poetry, at the time the most widely respected translator of Japanese literature before Arthur Waley. Chamberlain's *Classical Poetry of the Japanese* (1880) was the first study of Japanese poetry in a European language. Reprinted and combined with *Bashô and the Japanese Poetical Epigram* as *Japanese Poetry* (1910), Chamberlain's rhymed translations remained in print. Both works included descriptions and translations from Noh. Chamberlain was also a likely source of Pound's information about *hokku*, partly expressed when he wrote that in Japanese poetry one finds 'the expression, in natural language, of the simple feelings common to all' and instead of religion or moralising 'nothing but that hopeless sense of the transitoriness of life'. John Gould Fletcher may have recommended Chamberlain to Pound.[48] Additionally, Chamberlain became a source on the Noh acknowledged by both Pound and Yeats. Fenollosa, in fact, elaborates on Chamberlain's equation of the lyric drama of Japan with the drama of classical Greece.

The winter of 1913/14 was Pound's first with Yeats at Stone Cottage. Working with the Japanese materials on the Noh in the Fenollosa collection led to Pound's version of 'Nishikigi' appearing in *Poetry* in May 1914 and 'The Classical Drama of Japan' in the October 1914 issue of the *Quarterly Review*. Pound gradually suggested that the structure of Noh offered a way to imagine a 'long imagiste or vorticist poem'. Early in 1915 at the Café Royal, Pound met the dancer Michio Itô and then Itô's friend, the painter Kume. They partly helped with his work on Noh by dancing, visualising principles he was addressing in the drama. During this period – 1913 and 1914 – Japanese poetry and art were important models in the development of Pound's Imagist and Vorticist poetic as the critic David Ewick has demonstrated.[49]

As Giles' *History of Chinese Literature* introduced Pound to Chinese writing, W.G. Aston's *History of Japanese Literature* (1899) did the same for Japanese.

Aston's work on Japanese literature, like Giles on Chinese, emphasised European language translations of East Asian verse stressing that it was largely rhymed and tightly-metred – fitting English rather than Japanese poetics. Pound, of course, sought to correct this reading.

One other important figure was Arthur Waley, who also worked in the Department of Prints and Drawings at the British Museum before beginning a career at the School of Oriental and African Studies. Waley became part of Pound's circle, regularly invited to 5 Holland Park Chambers, Kensington, for Thursday night assemblies. These meetings would often include H.D., Richard Aldington, May Sinclair, Wyndham Lewis, Ford Madox Hueffer (later Ford), T.S. Eliot, Edmond Dulac and occasionally Yeats. Years later this group would expand and meet regularly on Mondays at a restaurant on Frith Street in Soho. What Pound would repeatedly emphasise in his enthusiastic leadership of such gatherings is that 'art does not avoid universals, it strikes at them all the harder in that it strikes through particulars', a statement that implicitly expresses an Oriental as well as Imagist aesthetic.[50]

Waley's translations from Chinese and Japanese confirmed links between East Asian and Anglo-Irish modernism because his language and syntax emphasised English constructions, although with Oriental imagery. Anthologies often reprinted his accessible translations but they tended to be literal rather than imaginative. His name became synonymous in the public's view with China for Western readers, his work occasionally parodied by Lytton Strachey or mimicked in *Punch*.[51] Indeed, when Pound reviewed Waley's *One Hundred and Seventy Chinese Poems* (1918), he noted Waley's objection to translators like himself who focused on the 'general emotion of the poems, their atmosphere or intensity'. To Pound's dismay, Waley preferred 'direct verbal meanings'.[52]

Waley published a booklet entitled *Chinese Poems* in December 1916 with copies sent to Pound, Binyon, T.S. Eliot and Iris Barry. Later, *One Hundred and Seventy Chinese Poems* appeared, followed by *Nō Plays of Japan* (1921). In 1923 he published an *Introduction to the Study of Chinese Painting* dedicated to Binyon. His *Tale of Genji*, the eleventh century masterpiece written by the noblewoman Murasaki Shikibu, often called the world's first novel, appeared in six volumes in English (1921–33) condensed to one in 1935. Waley favoured elaborate prose over accuracy: when he found an obscure or boring passage, he skipped it. He compensated for the vagueness of the original Japanese by substituting something equally lyrical in English. His version remained the most widely read translation from Japanese literature for generations, praised by Binyon, Yeats and Pound.[53]

Pound's belief that Chinese art and poetry embodied

elements of Imagist poetics and that China was the example of Confucian moral and political principles furthered his interest in the Orient. But Imagism was central. The British critic and poet T.E. Hulme first explored the contrast between the sensory image and traditional diction that led to isolating the image as the only poetic force in a Japanese or Chinese poem. Poetry, Hulme wrote, is not a language counter to prose 'but a visual, concrete one . . . It always endeavours to arrest you and to make you continuously see a physical thing, to prevent you gliding through an abstract process.' Poetry is a direct language because it deals in images. The natural object, Pound would soon write, 'is always the *adequate symbol*'.[54] Verbal concreteness is the goal in what became Pound's effort to modernise Orientalism and at the same time Orientalise modernism.[55]

Pound believed that, embedded in the Chinese poems glossed in the notebooks of Fenollosa, he had found validation of the principles he had been urging for Imagism. The Chinese poems valued precise expression and exact visual images. Instead of fuzzy abstractions, they displayed clear-cut, observed detail and economy of language which he had tried to initiate through Imagist poetry. Fenollosa's 'The Chinese Written Character as a Medium for Poetry', unpublished during his lifetime, further summarised and confirmed Pound's poetic doctrine. Edited by Pound and appearing in 1919, the essay articulated a series of practices Pound had been promoting. Now he could show an older origin for these ideas from a complimentary, if unfamiliar, culture.

Pound found his three tenets of Imagist poetry – direct treatment of the thing, use of absolutely 'no word that does not contribute to the presentation' and compositions in 'sequence of the musical phrase, not in sequence of the metronome' – in the work of Li Bai and others.[56] Imagists rejected sentiment and discursive writing; economy of language was the new goal plus experiments with verse, while isolating a single image as Pound did in 'In a Station of the Metro':

> The apparition of these faces in the crowd;
> Petals on a wet, black bough.

For Pound, *Cathay* was an Imagist text proving that such writing had been practised centuries earlier.

Elkin Mathews, the publisher of Yeats, Wilde, Arthur Symonds, Joyce and members of the Rhymers Club, soon became Pound's publisher. In late 1908 he published the second impression of Pound's second book, *A Quinzaine for this Yule*, following this with *Personae* (1909 and something of a popular success) and *Exultations* (1909) before *Canzoni* (1911). The next volume was *Cathay*.

11

Cathay: The Poems

In the Autumn of 1914, the poet H.D., living at 5 Holland Place Chambers, across the hall from Pound and Dorothy, vividly reported that Pound was absorbed in Chinese translations: 'some are very beautiful!' she noted and 'he comes running in four or five times a day now with new versions for us to read.'[57] Pound's enthusiasm for his Chinese work was infectious and he was eager to share it, although not with Fenollosa had he been alive. To Yeats' father, the painter Jack Yeats, Pound expressed thanks that Fenollosa was dead, adding that 'I should have had *the* hell of a time" trying to edit him living.'[58]

By 1914 Pound appeared to have found a language suitable for Chinese poetry. Later, in a written response to her review of *Lustra* (which included *Cathay*), he told Kate Buss, an American journalist and admirer, that 'all the verbal constructions of *Cathay* [were] already tried in "Provincia Deserta"'.[59] That poem, appearing first in *Poetry* in 1915 and then in *Lustra*, displays the controlled, precise line seen in *Cathay*, incorporating both Imagist and Chinese elements seen in the directness of the opening:

At Rochecoart,
Where the hills part
               in three ways,
And three valleys, full of winding roads,
Fork out to south and north,
There is a place of trees . . . gray with lichen.

In the poem, the narrator retells Provençal stories of battle and love with clarity: 'I have seen the fields, pale, clear as an emerald,/ Sharp peaks, high spurs, distant castles' and concludes with 'I have walked over these roads;/ I have thought of them living'.[60]

Of course, Pound writes this without mentioning his experiments in translating Chinese verse, nor his broad education in Japanese visual arts, nor his reading and study of the Orient. He was, indeed, inventing; as Eliot wrote several years later, 'Chinese poetry, as we know it today, is something invented by Ezra Pound' who has enriched 'modern English poetry as FitzGerald [translator of the *Rubaiyat of Omar Khayyam*] enriched it'.[61]

But the invention, occurring in the metrics, as well as allusions, images and forms of Pound's translations, is, according to Eliot, also 'a phase in the development of Pound's poetry'. To consider Pound's 'original work and his translation separately would be a mistake'.[62]

Pound reworked Fenollosa's materials using a *vers libre* method based on the notebooks' line-by-line version departing from Fenollosa's translation to create new poems of his own. More specifically, *vers libre* is a poetic form that eliminates consistent metre, rhyme or other patterns. It follows the rhythm of natural speech, creating an original if complicated metrical form for each poem. Flexibility of expression is its goal with the strophe, not the foot or number of syllables, the key unit. Unrhymed cadence built on organic rhythm, not a strict metrical system, rules. Denying a regular number of syllables as the basis of versification is its trademark. It began in France with the critic/journalist Gustave Kahn and poets like Baudelaire, Verlaine, Rimbaud, Mallarmé and Laforgue. The nature of Pound's 'free verse' method for the poems, bold and innovative, would surprise but influence contemporaries and many later poets.

Fenollosa's method in translating Chinese was to work from Japanese versions, written or 'translated' by Mori Kainan and Ariga Nagao. Pound worked in a similar style, relying, at least for knowledge of Chinese art and writing, on the Sinologists Binyon, Waley and the

American poet John Gould Fletcher, who was engaged in his own renditions of Chinese poetry. Pound's choice of Japanese names for Chinese poets – Rihaku instead of Li Bai for example – indicates the cultural mediation at work from Chinese to Japanese to English. With his Japanese assistants, Fenollosa had worked out the Japanese equivalents of the Chinese characters. Describing his early engagement with the material, Pound wrote to his father that he had 'busted into Fenollosa's chinese notes. – (not Japanese.) & found some fine stuff. that has kept me going for the past ten days.' That was in November 1914; a month later he reported that he 'got a good little book out of Fenollosa's Chinese notes'.[63] Pound was satisfied with what he had done. He knew it successfully joined Chinese and English poetry in imaginative ways. Mathews agreed to publish it immediately under the title of *Cathay*.

Yet even though he allowed himself complete freedom with the new texts, Pound's own voice is absent, preferring a variety of persona such as that of the young woman in 'The River-Merchant's Wife: a Letter'. The use of another voice was an early technique of Pound's, borrowed from Browning and used as the title of his 1909 collection, *Personae*. The verses of *Cathay* themselves celebrate Pound's self-effacement and sustain a dramatic quality of individual voices that help to establish their poetic excellence.

Ironically, the effect of *Cathay* may have been greatest on Pound. He considered the poems an extension of his own work, not simply as a collection of Chinese translations, as the insertion of 'The Seafarer' confirmed, but as an expression of the Imagist aesthetic. The opportunity to complete Fenollosa's project became a means of expanding himself as a poet and exposing himself to new creative possibilities. The volume, for all its effort at translation, is a book of poems by Ezra Pound. In documenting the provenance of the materials in the first edition, Pound included an opening sentence of descending spacing to look like poetry on the title page. Following 'CATHAY/ TRANSLATIONS by EZRA POUND' is:

FOR THE MOST PART FROM THE CHINESE
OF RIHAKU, FROM THE NOTES OF THE
LATE ERNEST FENOLLOSA, AND
THE DECIPHERINGS OF THE
PROFESSORS MORI
AND ARIGA

There are, then, four author/translators who precede Pound, who seemingly minimises his role as translator. The work, he implies, is a collaboration. An afterword to the first edition again qualifies Pound as a translator suggesting that further unpublished works remain unpublished because his skills are not adequate to do the proper translation. Yet he does cite four lines from the unpublished material including the line 'Drawing sword, cut into water, water again flow'. Diverting attention from his abilities as a translator, he adds that the 'personal hatred in which I am held by many' would spoil the reception of the poems,[64] a curious *ad hominem* remark suggesting animosity toward his project. He again repeats that he has published only a fraction of the Chinese poems available to him.

Still, the controversy surrounding the unorthodox translations of *Cathay* largely overshadowed reception of the book. Pound had rendered these classical Chinese poems without any knowledge of the source language. Complicating the matter was that the notebooks often did not include Chinese characters offering only the Japanese pronunciation of the lines in the Chinese poems. The journey from Chinese to Japanese to English resulted in uneven English. Faults occurred throughout this line of transmission, although they did not deter Pound from revising or 'translating' the poems with a new focus on the complete image of a text rather than just reproducing details in the original work.

Up until this moment, Pound's efforts as a translator focused on languages with which he had some formal knowledge: Italian for Cavalcanti, Provençal for Arnaut Daniel and Anglo-Saxon for 'The Seafarer'.

The intercession of two Japanese professors mark his and Fenollosa's ignorance of Chinese, although Pound fitfully began to study it after *Cathay* appeared. With characteristic enthusiasm, he soon celebrated Chinese as *the* language to study suggesting it should replace Greek in academic curricula. He quickly went on to celebrate Fenollosa's 'Ideogramic Method' in 'The Chinese Written Character as a Medium for Poetry'. Juxtaposition of image and idea without abstract argument or logical connections, stressing implied mental relationships, shortly became an important principle of Pound's modernism. Pound admitted there was conflict between the philological and the aesthetic in his translations but, as Wai-lim Yip writes, even given the barest of details Pound is 'able to get into the central consciousness of the original'.[65]

Pound repeatedly prioritised the poetic over the semantic in translating, a habit learned through his imagist practice. 'Don't bother about the WORDS, translate the MEANING' he advised a potential translator. Translation was a collaborative practice as Hugh Kenner explained: for Pound 'translation was a model for a poetic act: blood brought to ghosts.'[66] Sinologists were, nonetheless, horrified and mistakes occurred. For example, Pound conflated two separate poems by Li Bai into 'The River Song'. Part of this and other errors may have derived from misrepresentations attributable to Mori's flawed summaries and Fenollosa's rough translations. But in his re-workings, Pound also corrected a considerable number of errors as in 'Lament of the Frontier Guard' as Wai-lim Yip has shown.[67] In 'Exile's Letter' and 'The River-Merchant's Wife', Pound went beyond Fenollosa's fragmented notes and captured much of the original poetic energy largely because he focused on reproducing the whole image, not just local details. The poetics of reticence triumphed in both the original and Pound's translations.

Unfortunately, critics were not restrained in their responses: Pound, as one critic wrote, is 'a true radical in his devotion to veritism, in his regard for the anatomy of poetry and his contempt for mere verbal upholstery.' Other readers were equally responsive, A.R. Orage, editor of the *New Age*, explained that the poems have a pure content, that is 'perfectly natural', matched by a form 'equally *perfectly* natural – that is delicately regularized, selected, artistic.' The *Times Literary Supplement* called the poems 'sharp and precise', while Ford Madox Ford referred to them as 'things of supreme beauty'. With Orage, Ford believed the book to be the best Pound had yet done.[68] Wyndham Lewis in *Blast 2* claimed that Pound was the 'demon pantechnicon driver, busy with removal of old world into new quarters. In his steel net of impeccable technique he has lately caught Li Po [Li Bai]. Energy of a discriminating element.'[69]

A review in the *Bookman* of July 1915 comments on the multiple but diffuse methods of translating Chinese poetry from rhymed and unrhymed couplets and stanzas of various kinds. But Pound sought 'for an honesty of method. His translations are not mere excuses' but works that offer the 'fastidious colours of Chinese art', in many ways a perceptive remark since it acknowledges Pound's visual awareness of Chinese painting.[70]

The issue, however, was whether *Cathay* was a collection of translations or a set of original poems and many have taken Pound to task for his inadequate or false translations.[71] T.S. Eliot, however, took a less inflammatory view, claiming in his introduction to the *Selected Poems* (1928), that Pound was not only 'the inventor of Chinese poetry for our time' but that 'each generation must translate for itself'.[72] The volume achieved a new voice for poetry, which even George Steiner in his comprehensive study of translation *After Babel* praised. The poems in *Cathay*, he wrote, 'altered the feel of the language and set the pattern of cadence for modern verse.'[73] *Cathay* introduced Chinese poetry to twentieth century readers, achieving an elegant simplicity by disregarding the rhymes and tones, while recreating their methods of presentation.

In his 1918 essay 'Chinese Poetry', Pound attempts to elide the differences between Chinese and European poetry. He implies that what he chose to publish in

Cathay are Chinese poems displaying Western attributes. He cites 'The Jewel Stairs' Grievance' and 'The River-Merchant's Wife: a Letter' as articulating Western qualities in Chinese verse. The latter is also an example of epistolary poetics, making a subtle comparison to the work of Browning:

> It is interesting to find, in eighth-century China, a
> poem which might have been slipped into Browning's
> work without causing any surprise save by its
> simplicity and its naïve beauty.[74]

The Chinese, he adds, have a long tradition of the dramatic monologue. But Pound is also critical of the way we have read as well as translated Chinese poetry. In 'The Chinese Written Character' essay of 1919, speaking through the words of Fenollosa, he writes that 'we import into our reading of Chinese all the weakness of our own formalisms'.[75] We have mistakenly replaced the flexibility of words and approach needed for Chinese writing with fixed ideas of correct expression and form. The context of Pound's comment on reading Chinese poetry is important for it displays both inherited somewhat rigid attitudes and new ways of conceiving what was also called 'the Middle Kingdom'.

Contrasting with Pound's traditional if somewhat clichéd concept of 'Cathay' was his experimental verse expressed in imagery and syntax in the poems of *Cathay*. The basic tension in the collection is, in fact, that between the world imagined by the conventional term 'Cathay' and the originality of Pound's English text.

Cathay's impact on the practice of English translations of East Asian verse, usually rhymed and tightly metered, was lasting. After *Cathay*, such translations seemed unnatural and ill-suited to Chinese poetry, John Gould Fletcher and others argued. Pound's free verse style 'made it new'. Even Yeats acknowledged this advance. In his 'Introduction' to the *Oxford Book of Modern Verse 1892–1935*, Yeats wrote that Pound's *Cathay* 'created the manner followed with more learning but with less subtlety of rhythm by Arthur Waley in many volumes.'[76] In the anthology, Yeats included, as the first of four selections from Pound, 'The River-Merchant's Wife: a Letter'. Waley's translation 'The Temple' by Po-Chü-i of the Tang Dynasty followed.

Another feature of Pound's undertaking is that as Fenollosa relied on various redactions from the Chinese to Japanese to English, Pound duplicated the process as he began the early stages of *The Cantos*. Pound relied on histories, details, resources and even the research of others in writing *The Cantos*, some of it incorporated into the text, much the way Fenollosa relied on the various transcriptions and translations from his two assistants.

One critical example: the same year he wrote *Cathay*, Pound made a translation of the *Nekuia*, the land-of-the dead episode from Homer's *Odyssey*, which would eventually become the first of *The Cantos*. To complete it, he went not to an early Greek source but to Andreas Divus's Latin version of 1538. He then introduced a metre based not on Greek or even Italian but Anglo-Saxon. Pound was likely aware of the parallel to Fenollosa's process because several letters show that he originally intended to publish both works in the same volume.[77] In terms of method, *Cathay* was a prototype.

But what poets did Pound translate in *Cathay*? And why these fourteen poems, selected from almost 150 in Fenollosa's notebooks? The answer to the first question is clear, the second not so. However, the order of the published poems is itself telling with Rihaku clearly the pivot around which the other figures circle. The order is:

Kutsugen (Ka-Gi), 'Song of the Bowmen of Shu'
The oldest poem in the collection ca. 1100 BCE according to Fenollosa's notes and found in the Book of Songs attributed to Confucius.

Mei Sheng, 'The Beautiful Toilet'
This poem, like the first, works by direct observation; attention to detail alone generates emotion of the

neglected courtesan. The writing is objective.

Rihaku (Li Bai), 'The River Song'
Opulent in imagery and sensuality; realism is diminished; Emperor departs with his imperial guards to inspect his flowers, not his troops. The Emperor is idle.

Rihaku, 'The River-Merchant's Wife: a Letter'
A direct and intimate poem with objective description that explores the theme of loyalty during separation as in 'Song of The Bowmen of Shu'.

Rihaku, 'The Jewel Stairs' Grievance'
A poem about a second neglected court lady.

Rihaku, 'Poem by the Bridge at Ten-Shin'
Decadence at court as in 'The River Song'; regret for old days.

Rihaku, 'Lament of the Frontier Guard'
A poem about the sorrow of war.

Rihaku, 'Exile's Letter'
Explores the theme of exile which dominates part two of the collection. An elegiac tone emerges.

Anglo-Saxon poet, 'The Seafarer'
Pound argued it was written at approximately the same

time as 'Exile's Letter' in the eighth century but the two
views, one of eighth century China and the other of
Anglo-Saxon England, contrast. The former represents a
decadent world, the latter a heroic one.

From Rihaku, 'Four Poems of Departure':
'Separation the River Kiang'
'Taking Leave of a Friend'
'Leave-taking near Shoku'
'The City of Choan'
Poems of loss, departure and longing.

'South-Folk in Cold Country'
A third war poem about the waste and hardships of war.[78]

Absent from the list is any work titled 'Cathay'.

Three short sentences provide front matter for the volume. They precede the first poem, 'Song of the Bowmen of Shu' and read:

Rihaku flourished in the eighth century of our era.
The Anglo-Saxon Seafarer is of about this period.
The other poems from the Chinese are earlier.[79]

This is a short defence of Pound's odd decision to include his translation of the Old English 'Seafarer', a poem he later removed when the volume was reprinted.

He possibly included it to display, first, his extended ability as a translator and second because he wanted to demonstrate the historical nexus between the work of Rihaku and the unknown Anglo-Saxon poet. He also wanted to show parallels and similarities between Oriental and Anglo-Saxon writing.

Yet the presence and placement of 'The Seafarer' is important. Positioned almost in the middle of Pound's finished text of the fourteen poems in the first edition, his earlier translation of the Anglo-Saxon poem appears between 'Exile's Letter' and 'Four Poems of Departure'. This is likely to emphasise the contemporaneity of the ancient Tang Dynasty and Anglo-Saxon culture. Both societies are parallel in their use of political power to dismiss those out of favour or who pose a threat, the condition of the two protagonists. Pound also believed that the two poems were written at the same time and function comparatively, joining East and West, while adding a topical dimension: war, which links it to the 'Song of the Bowmen of Shu' and 'Lament of the Frontier Guard'.

Interestingly, Pound sent these war poems to his friend the sculptor Gaudier-Brzeska who was at the front during the First World War and would be killed in battle, a death which devastated Pound. The 'Exile's Letter', and 'The Seafarer' link the themes of exile and battle in *Cathay*, as well as the situation in Europe in 1915. Pound originally published 'The Seafarer' in the

New Age of 30 November 1911, long before meeting Mary Fenollosa and conceiving *Cathay*.[80] He felt it belonged in the new text, but when he republished *Cathay*, as a section of *Lustra*, five additional poems from the notebooks appeared; 'The Seafarer' did not.[81]

A defensive note by Pound on the last page of *Cathay* stating that there are more poems helps to answer the second question above: he chose the works he translated because he believed them to be 'unquestionable poems', that is the finest in the Fenollosa notebooks. He was also under the sway of Vorticism, the English avant-garde movement initiated by Wyndham Lewis and Pound that focused on geometric forms and hard-edged imagery derived from machines. He believed that the poems of *Cathay* exhibited certain similarities to those of Vorticism. In his 1918 essay 'Chinese Poetry', Pound explained that he translated Chinese poetry because of its qualities of 'vivid presentation' and because the poets 'have been content to set forth their matter without moralizing and without comment'.[82] In a sense, hard-edged.

In practical terms, for other poems not in the volume, notably 'Five Colour Screen' by Rihaku, which Pound calls a type of *Ars Poetica* ('Art of Poetry', the title of a work by the classical poet Horace), line breaks for explanation and notes would be needed. Furthermore, contempt for his free approach to translation and censure over his declared belief in certain young artists, would likely be brought to bear on the flaws of such translation and would likely deprecate the entire volume. He would take no such risk.[83]

The freedom of not knowing Chinese allowed Pound to display his own strengths as a poet and develop the line as the unit of composition, noticeable in 'The Beautiful Toilet' by Mei Sheng of the Han Fu school, the second poem in *Cathay*. It opens with:

> Blue, blue is the grass about the river
> And the willows have overfilled the close garden.
> And within, the mistress, in the midmost of her
>   youth,
> White, white of face, hesitates, passing the door.
> Slender, she puts forth a slender hand,

But the imagistic setting with its concentrated focus on the grass, the willows and the white face of the mistress, suddenly turns dramatic when we read in the final four line stanza:

> And she was a courtezan in the old days,
> And she has married a sot,
> Who now goes drunkenly out
> And leaves her too much alone.[84]

This is as if Mei Sheng, the poet of most likely the first

century CE, and the Victorian Browning have united. Loneliness and claustrophobia compete both in the description and in verses that introduced the shorter, five-character line to Chinese poetry followed for many centuries.

Importantly, many of the techniques and sensibility displayed in *Cathay* soon found their way in to *The Cantos* as this short passage from Canto 13 illustrates:

> The blossoms of the apricot
>> blow from the east to the west,
> And I have tried to keep them from falling.

Here, image and action by Kung (Confucius) join in the attenuated movement of the apricot blossoms. Throughout *The Cantos*, Pound incorporates metre and image introduced in *Cathay*. His creation of the so-called 'Seven Lakes Canto' (Canto 49), a blend of Orientalism and American pastoralism, further reflects the presence of *Cathay*, or at least its style, in the text, supplanted by Confucius in the so-called China Cantos (Cantos 52–61).[85] There, Pound presents the dynastic history of China as a struggle between harmonic Imperial rule based on Confucian principles and forces of corruption from outside and inside the country. The source for his material was the thirteen-volume *Histoire Générale de la Chine* by Joseph de Maillé, a French Jesuit in the eighteenth century Chinese court. The first of various Chinese ideograms Pound introduces in *The Cantos* appears at the end of Canto 51 immediately before the opening of the Chinese Cantos.

The second line of the 'Seven Lakes Canto' – 'Rain; empty river; a voyage' – is almost pure *Cathay*, the poetic and linguistic conventions establishing an Orientalist setting and mood. Brief lines rely on alliteration and assonance, not rhyme: 'Where wine flag catches the sunset/ Sparse chimneys smoke in the cross light.' Controlled observation, seen throughout *Cathay*, dominates. Time slows down with the minimal use of verbs in favour of nouns and adjectives. The result is concentrated attention on physical detail duplicating the method of *Cathay* which remains formative throughout *The Cantos*.

At times the often monotonous movement of lines in *Cathay*, with repetitious phrasing and repeated syntactical patterns, intentionally give the poems an archaic quality possibly anticipated by readers in 1915. Such a structure would fulfil their stereotypical view of Oriental writing. But Pound contrasts this with his precise, sharp and exact imagery, structure and language in conflict to fashion a unique text. Another disruption is that the poems labelled song are hardly songs: they lack the lyrical, eloquent manner of the English song seen as early as the first anthology of English poems, *Songs and Sonnets* (1557) printed by Richard Tottel. Sir Philip Sydney, Thomas Wyatt, Edmund Spenser and Shakespeare exemplify the form of the English poetic song largely inherited from Petrarch. The Chinese definition of poem, *shige*, is absent in Pound. *Shi* means poem, *ge* means song so in Chinese, poems and poem-songs are interchangeable definitions. Nevertheless, Pound alludes generally to the English tradition despite seeking to be true to the sense and meaning of what the original authors intended, rather than what would make clear sense to an English reader.[86]

The language of the opening poem, 'Song of the Bowmen of Shu', demonstrates this clearly. It takes us back to origins, something almost primitive, which is Pound's point. The language is simple but direct and intense:

> Here we are, picking the first fern-shoots
> And saying: When shall we get back to our
>   country?
>
> . . .
>
> We have no comfort because of these Mongols.[87]

In *Cathay* Pound displayed a technical versatility, mastering *vers libre* as shown in both the short and long lines seen in 'The River Merchant's Wife: a Letter':

At sixteen you departed,

You went into far Ku-to-Yen, by the river of swirl-
ing eddies,

And you have been gone five months.

. . .

The leaves fall early this autumn, in wind.

The paired butterflies are already yellow with
August[.][88]

The alternating lines express alternating emotions, both
for the subject and the reader.

Thematically, *Cathay* unites a consistent emotional
outlook with a persistent tone of loss, expressed suc-
cinctly at the end of 'Song of the Bowmen of Shu' and in
'Exile's Letter' as in the line 'What is the use of talking . . .
There is no end of things in the heart.'[89] The volume,
according to the critic Ron Bush, is a meditation on
isolation and the inability of even language to relieve it.
Fighting, separation, departure and exile dominate the
text with Imperial China displayed in political as well
as military disarray.[90] Wars, battles and fighting such as
the War of Eight Princes (291–306) or the later armed
conquests of the Tang Dynasty (618–907) lead to con-
tinual conflict and upheaval. Indeed, two of the poems
in *Cathay* are letters which, because of the vicissitudes
of conflict, may or may not have been received.

111

Impact and Importance

In contrast to the erratic, often critical reaction to *The Cantos*, and despite the outcry of Chinese scholars, *Cathay* received almost universal acclaim when first published. Nevertheless, its inaccuracies and errors in translation created a firestorm of criticism, ranging from Pound's lack of respect for the texts he adapted to an attack on what he 'considered to be the current poetic demise by using a foreign force'.[91] But it won praise as poetry, not as translation; its canonical status would go on to overshadow Pound's uneven later epic.

The small format thirty-two page *Cathay* appeared in April 1915 at the price of one shilling. Dominating the tan paper front cover in bold black ink on the left was the Chinese character or ideogram for radiance or brilliance 耀 pronounced *yào*. Pound may have located it in notes for 'The Chinese Written Character as a Medium for Poetry'. Dropped down on the bottom right of the cover in small capitals is 'CATHAY' and below that moved slightly to the right and in a somewhat smaller font is 'EZRA POUND'. Mathews printed one thousand copies of *Cathay*, supplementing that (and enhancing Pound's visibility) with 2000 copies of an advertisement leaflet to publicise the book. That same month he also printed a fourth issue of Pound's *Ripostes*, originally published in 1912.[92]

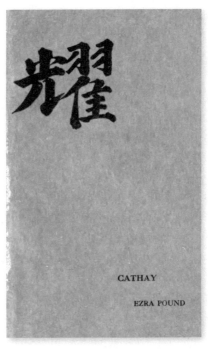

First edition cover, 1915

Pound assembled the book at the beginning of World War I, while London began to suffer from German strategic bombing raids often by Zeppelin airships; both civilian casualties and fear mounted. The very day *Cathay* appeared, two German naval airships headed to London but had to divert because of bad weather. Initially, the first sequence of twelve poems of *Cathay* contained only one about war, 'Song of the Bowmen of Shu'. But before going to press and perhaps because the war was intensifying, Pound added 'Lament of the Frontier Guard' and 'South-Fork in Cold Country' to augment an anti-war theme. Readers would immediately identify with the anxiety and anguish of the Frontier Guard as he climbs 'the towers and towers/ to watch out the barbarous land / Desolate castle, the sky, the wide desert./ There is no wall left to this village'.[93] Pound appended four more poems with similar themes when he later incorporated the book into *Lustra*.

Exile, as well as war, emerges in the text. Absorbing Taoist qualities of the original poetry, which emphasised authorial detachment allowing the images to speak for themselves, the poems express the nature of separation and exile. This is also a feature of Taoist poetry which seeks 'to express incompleteness in an effort to be complete in the moment.'[94] Exiled East Asian scholar-officials such as Su Shi, Meng Haoran and Li Bai, with political careers in ruin, would compose poems based on their feelings of separation from their families and shattered heroism.

Overall reception of the book in the past one hundred years, beginning with the Imagist John Gould Fletcher, has emphasised its significance as a book of original works by Pound rather than strict translations from the Chinese. Fletcher outlined Pound's innovations in 'The Orient and Contemporary Poetry' beginning with his avoidance of a strict metrical scheme, ignoring the rhymes and tones of Chinese for the power of the image. According to David Ewick, Fletcher actually saw an early draft of *Cathay* in the winter of 1914–1915.[95] The focus on imagery, natural events and things in themselves, concrete images and objects, were the elements that resonated with Pound's contemporaries and successors.

A counterweight to the opacity and ambiguity of much modernist poetry, Pound's translations express an aesthetic of clarity which is the core of his writing, even though in his later work he would be distracted by history and economics.

The most celebrated poem in *Cathay*, 'The River-Merchant's Wife: a Letter', has, in particular, been admired for its restraint, while combining repressed passion with humility. The poem opens with:

While my hair was still cut straight across my
    forehead

I played about the front gate, pulling flowers.

You came by on bamboo stilts, playing horse,

You walked about my seat, playing with blue plums.

And we went on living in the village of Chokan:

Two small people, without dislike or suspicion.[96]

The language sets up the drama to come as an element of displeasure and suspicion that will shortly enter the world of the River-Merchant's wife. Kenneth Rexroth, not a fan of Pound's, nonetheless offered high praise for the work as one of the 'dozen or so major poems to be written by an American in the twentieth century, and still the best single translation from the Chinese.'[97] Even Yip admits that the better Sinologist Waley cannot match the intuitive understanding found in Pound's text which displays translation as transformation.

One of Pound's strategies in *Cathay* is to invent Chinese by de-familiarising his English, possibly a defence of his not knowing Chinese and never having dealt with Chinese characters directly. The line 'At morning there are flowers to cut the heart', from 'Poem by the Bridge at Ten-Shin', maintains the texture of linguistic strangeness as he transcribes almost literally a note of Fenollosa's.[98] Pound's phrasing also recaptures an earlier state in the progress of language and Fenollosa's belief that Chinese poems must feel their way back to linguistic origins through individual words which like Greek are concrete, direct and monosyllabic. As Robert Kern observes, at this time writing for Pound is 'a process of stripping words of their associations in order to arrive at their exact meanings . . . presenting arrangements of language that emphasise their own strangeness with respect to more conventional . . . modes of expression.'[99] This relates to Pound's concept of the image, defined as 'that which presents an intellectual and emotional complex in an instant of time.'[100] The poems in *Cathay*, while repeatedly demonstrating 'their [own] foreignness', also repeatedly present the image in all of its complexity.[101]

Pound's work is also a formative event in the move toward collaborative translation. His unique, free 'translations', expressed in new forms of Imagist poetry, adjusted to the nuances of Chinese as he understood the language, are works of true originality. Not all readers agreed but *Cathay*'s creativity has remained a goal for many poets who followed. But while he insistently called his work a 'translation', Pound also suggests the uncertainty of his undertaking in a tone of self-assurance if not overstatement: 'I have not come to the end of Ernest Fenollosa's notes by a long way, nor is it entirely perplexity that causes me to cease from translation.'[102] There are many other works, but he hesitates to include them.

The impact of China on Pound stuck to him. But outside of a small literary circle, for the most part the West did not get it. In 1935, Pound would complain that 'the whole Occident is still in crass ignorance of the Chinese art of verbal sonority. I now doubt if it was inferior to the Greek.' A BBC film taken of him in the 1960s shows him carefully explaining to the camera the pictorial relation between the Chinese characters for sun, wood and east. The idea first surfaced in an essay he edited and published in 1918, 'Chinese Poetry'. As he elaborated earlier in *The Spirit of Romance*, 'the spirit of the arts is dynamic,' alive, vibrant and always changing.[103]

Sato's Sword

The importance of Orientalism in the work of other major poets of the time might be best symbolised by the story of Sato's sword. This was an ancient 550-year-old Japanese sword presented to Yeats in 1920 by Junzō Sato, the Japanese consul in Portland, Oregon. Yeats was on tour and Sato, who had read his work in Japan, visited the poet to present him with the majestic heirloom after hearing Yeats speak. Yeats initially declined the gift but had to accept it because to refuse would embarrass if not insult Sato. He later wrote to Sato that the sword would be returned to him upon Yeats's death. The poet soon incorporated the 'changeless sword' in 'My Table' in 'Meditations in Time of Civil War' with further references in 'A Dialogue Between Self and Soul' and 'Symbols'. He also dedicated his play *The Resurrection* to Sato.

In 'My Table', the sword acts to motivate Yeats, stimulating him to shake his 'days out of their aimlessness'. It reminds him of what his poetry should be and his role as an artist creating disciplined, timeless poetry. The sword integrates the lasting values of the Orient expressed in *Cathay* with western poetry, values of continuity, history, respect and well-structured art. Given by Sato to Yeats, it marks a passing from the world of the East to that of the West, occurring symbolically in the New World, America. By extension, it re-confirms the importance of Pound's Chinese poems 'translated' from not one but two languages. The sword represents the transnational qualities of family, history and ideals as do the poems of *Cathay* which embody the foundational techniques Pound would incorporate in *The Cantos* expressed in the paratactic lines of the 'Seven Lakes Canto'. The three categories established in 'Rain; empty river; a voyage,' underscore the movement, contrast and journeying needed to make the experience of the 'Seven Lakes Canto' whole; as a result, the divisions between East and West evaporate, creating, as the poem concludes, 'the dimension of stillness./ And the power over wild beasts' (Canto 49).

In his essay 'Chinese Poetry', Pound outlined the poetic features he found lacking in the West: the Chinese '*like* poetry that they have to think about', something seen only in twelfth century Provence and thirteenth century Tuscany. Next, there is a 'directness and realism such as we find only in early Saxon verse and in the Poema del Cid and in Homer' who wrote without epithet. And finally, there is a 'simplicity and naïve beauty' matched by completeness.[104] Two lines from the 'Jewel Stairs' Grievance', and virtually all of *Cathay*, reflect these features:

And I let down the crystal curtain
And watch the moon through the clear autumn.[105]

Pound was a member of the transatlantic modernists who included Whistler, James, Eliot, Stein and later F. Scott Fitzgerald, Hemingway, Richard Wright and James Baldwin. But he grew beyond them to become a transnational modernist who never lost his interest in both Japan and China via art, Confucius and poetry. His late works, the *Confucian Analects* and *The Classic Anthology Defined by Confucius*, confirm his continued commitment to the East. Indeed, in 1945 when imprisoned by the U.S. Army in Pisa for treasonous radio broadcasts made on Italian radio beamed at the U.S., he spent part of his time translating Confucius. When his wife came to visit, he asked her to bring several ideograms from a Confucian text he did not have. Furthermore, when first arrested by Italian partisans and taken to the Americans, he slipped his Confucius text in his pocket along with a Chinese dictionary. For the next twenty-seven years, they rarely left his side.

APPENDIX

CATHAY, THE TEXT

CATHAY

EZRA POUND

CATHAY

TRANSLATIONS BY

EZRA POUND

FOR THE MOST PART FROM THE CHINESE
OF RIHAKU, FROM THE NOTES OF THE
LATE ERNEST FENOLLOSA, AND
THE DECIPHERINGS OF THE
PROFESSORS MORI
AND ARIGA

LONDON
ELKIN MATHEWS, CORK STREET
MCMXV

Rihaku flourished in the eighth century of our era.
The Anglo-Saxon Seafarer is of about this period.
The other poems from the Chinese are earlier.

Song of the Bowmen of Shu

HERE we are, picking the first fern-shoots
And saying: When shall we get back to our
    country?
Here we are because we have the Ken-nin for our
    foemen,
We have no comfort because of these Mongols.
We grub the soft fern-shoots,
When anyone says "Return," the others are full of
    sorrow.
Sorrowful minds, sorrow is strong, we are hungry
    and thirsty.
Our defence is not yet made sure, no one can let
    his friend return.
We grub the old fern-stalks.
We say: Will we be let to go back in October?
There is no ease in royal affairs, we have no comfort.
Our sorrow is bitter, but we would not return to our
    country.
What flower has come into blossom?
Whose chariot? The General's.
Horses, his horses even, are tired. They were strong.

We have no rest, three battles a month.

By heaven, his horses are tired.

The generals are on them, the soldiers are by them

The horses are well trained, the generals have ivory
    arrows and quivers ornamented with fish-
    skin.

The enemy is swift, we must be careful.

When we set out, the willows were drooping with
    spring,

We come back in the snow,

We go slowly, we are hungry and thirsty,

Our mind is full of sorrow, who will know of our
    grief?

By Kutsugen.
4th Century B.C.

The Beautiful Toilet

BLUE, blue is the grass about the river
And the willows have overfilled the close garden.
And within, the mistress, in the midmost of her
    youth,
White, white of face, hesitates, passing the door.
Slender, she puts forth a slender hand,

And she was a courtezan in the old days,
And she has married a sot,
Who now goes drunkenly out
And leaves her too much alone.

By Mei Sheng.
B.C. 140.

The River Song

THIS boat is of shato-wood, and its gunwales are
    cut magnolia,
Musicians with jewelled flutes and with pipes of gold
Fill full the sides in rows, and our wine
Is rich for a thousand cups.
We carry singing girls, drift with the drifting water,
Yet Sennin needs
A yellow stork for a charger, and all our seamen
Would follow the white gulls or ride them.
Kutsu's prose song
Hangs with the sun and moon.

King So's terraced palace
                      is now but a barren hill,
But I draw pen on this barge
Causing the five peaks to tremble,
And I have joy in these words
                 like the joy of blue islands.
(If glory could last forever
Then the waters of Han would flow northward.)

And I have moped in the Emperor's garden, await-
    ing an order-to-write !
I looked at the dragon-pond, with its willow-
    coloured water
Just reflecting the sky's tinge,
And heard the five-score nightingales aimlessly
    singing.

The eastern wind brings the green colour into the
    island grasses at Yei-shu,
The purple house and the crimson are full of Spring
    softness.
South of the pond the willow-tips are half-blue and
    bluer,
Their cords tangle in mist, against the brocade-like
    palace.
Vine-strings a hundred feet long hang down from
    carved railings,
And high over the willows, the fine birds sing to
    each other, and listen,
Crying—"Kwan, Kuan," for the early wind, and the
    feel of it.
The wind bundles itself into a bluish cloud and
    wanders off.
Over a thousand gates, over a thousand doors are
    the sounds of spring singing,

And the Emperor is at Ko.

Five clouds hang aloft, bright on the purple sky,

The imperial guards come forth from the golden
house with their armour a-gleaming.

The emperor in his jewelled car goes out to inspect
his flowers,

He goes out to Hori, to look at the wing-flapping
storks,

He returns by way of Sei rock, to hear the new
nightingales,

For the gardens at Jo-run are full of new nightingales,

Their sound is mixed in this flute,

Their voice is in the twelve pipes here.

By Rihaku.
8th century A.D.

The River-Merchant's Wife: a Letter

WHILE my hair was still cut straight across my
      forehead
I played about the front gate, pulling flowers.
You came by on bamboo stilts, playing horse,
You walked about my seat, playing with blue plums.
And we went on living in the village of Chokan:
Two small people, without dislike or suspicion.

At fourteen I married My Lord you.
I never laughed, being bashful.
Lowering my head, I looked at the wall.
Called to, a thousand times, I never looked back.

At fifteen I stopped scowling,
I desired my dust to be mingled with yours
Forever and forever, and forever.
Why should I climb the look out?

At sixteen you departed,
You went into far Ku-to-Yen, by the river of swirl-
      ing eddies,

And you have been gone five months.

The monkeys make sorrowful noise overhead.

You dragged your feet when you went out.

By the gate now, the moss is grown, the different
    mosses,

Too deep to clear them away!

The leaves fall early this autumn, in wind.

The paired butterflies are already yellow with
    August

Over the grass in the West garden,

They hurt me.

I grow older,

If you are coming down through the narrows of the
    river Kiang,

Please let me know beforehand,

And I will come out to meet you,

                    As far as Cho-fu-Sa.

                    By Rihaku.

The Jewel Stairs' Grievance

THE jewelled steps are already quite white with
    dew,
It is so late that the dew soaks my gauze stockings,
And I let down the crystal curtain
And watch the moon through the clear autumn.

By Rihaku.

NOTE.—Jewel stairs, therefore a palace. Grievance, therefore there is something to complain of. Gauze stockings,
therefore a court lady, not a servant who complains. Clear
autumn, therefore he has no excuse on account of weather.
Also she has come early, for the dew has not merely whitened
the stairs, but has soaked her stockings. The poem is especially prized because she utters no direct reproach.

Poem by the Bridge at Ten-Shin

MARCH has come to the bridge head,
Peach boughs and apricot boughs hang over a
      thousand gates,
At morning there are flowers to cut the heart,
And evening drives them on the eastward-flowing
      waters.
Petals are on the gone waters and on the going,
      And on the back-swirling eddies,
But to-day's men are not the men of the old days,
Though they hang in the same way over the bridge-
      rail.

The sea's colour moves at the dawn
And the princes still stand in rows, about the throne,
And the moon falls over the portals of Sei-go-yo,
And clings to the walls and the gate-top.
With head-gear glittering against the cloud and
      sun,
The lords go forth from the court, and into far
      borders.
They ride upon dragon-like horses,

Upon horses with head-trappings of yellow-metal,

And the streets make way for their passage.

              Haughty their passing,

Haughty their steps as they go into great banquets,

To high halls and curious food,

To the perfumed air and girls dancing,

To clear flutes and clear singing;

To the dance of the seventy couples;

To the mad chase through the gardens.

Night and day are given over to pleasure

And they think it will last a thousand autumns,

           Unwearying autumns.

For them the yellow dogs howl portents in vain,

And what are they compared to the lady Riokushu,

           That was cause of hate!

Who among them is a man like Han-rei

           Who departed alone with his mistress,

With her hair unbound, and he his own skiffs-man !

By Rihaku.

Lament of the Frontier Guard

By the North Gate, the wind blows full of sand,
Lonely from the beginning of time until now!
Trees fall, the grass goes yellow with autumn.
I climb the towers and towers
                    to watch out the barbarous land:
Desolate castle, the sky, the wide desert.
There is no wall left to this village.
Bones white with a thousand frosts,
High heaps, covered with trees and grass;
Who brought this to pass?
Who has brought the flaming imperial anger?
Who has brought the army with drums and with
        kettle-drums?
Barbarous kings.
A gracious spring, turned to blood-ravenous autumn,
A turmoil of wars-men, spread over the middle
        kingdom,
Three hundred and sixty thousand,
And sorrow, sorrow like rain.
Sorrow to go, and sorrow, sorrow returning,
Desolate, desolate fields,

And no children of warfare upon them,
     No longer the men for offence and defence.
Ah, how shall you know the dreary sorrow at the
     North Gate,
With Rihoku's name forgotten,
And we guardsmen fed to the tigers.

Rihaku.

Exile's Letter

To So-Kin of Rakuyo, ancient friend, Chancellor
    of Gen.
Now I remember that you built me a special tavern
By the south side of the bridge at Ten-Shin.
With yellow gold and white jewels, we paid for
    songs and laughter
And we were drunk for month on month, forget-
    ting the kings and princes.
Intelligent men came drifting in from the sea and
    from the west border,
And with them, and with you especially
There was nothing at cross purpose,
And they made nothing of sea-crossing or of
    mountain crossing,
If only they could be of that fellowship,
And we all spoke out our hearts and minds, and
    without regret.

And then I was sent off to South Wei,
             smothered in laurel groves,
And you to the north of Raku-hoku,

Till we had nothing but thoughts and memories in
   common.

And then, when separation had come to its worst,
We met, and travelled into Sen-Go,
Through all the thirty-six folds of the turning and
   twisting waters,
Into a valley of the thousand bright flowers,
That was the first valley;
And into ten thousand valleys full of voices and
   pine-winds.
And with silver harness and reins of gold,
Out come the East of Kan foreman and his
   company.
And there came also the "True man" of Shi-yo to
   meet me,
Playing on a jewelled mouth-organ.
In the storied houses of San-Ko they gave us more
   Sennin music,
Many instruments, like the sound of young phoenix
   broods.
The foreman of Kan Chu, drunk, danced
         because his long sleeves wouldn't keep still
With that music-playing.
And I, wrapped in brocade, went to sleep with my
   head on his lap,

And my spirit so high it was all over the heavens,
And before the end of the day we were scattered
        like stars, or rain.
I had to be off to So, far away over the waters,
You back to your river-bridge.

And your father, who was brave as a leopard,
Was governor in Hei Shu, and put down the bar-
        barian rabble.
And one May he had you send for me,
                despite the long distance.
And what with broken wheels and so on, I won't
        say it wasn't hard going,
Over roads twisted like sheeps' guts.
And I was still going, late in the year,
                in the cutting wind from the North,
And thinking how little you cared for the cost,
                and you caring enough to pay it.
And what a reception:
Red jade cups, food well set on a blue jewelled table,
And I was drunk, and had no thought of returning.
And you would walk out with me to the western
        corner of the castle,
To the dynastic temple, with water about it clear
        as blue jade,

With boats floating, and the sound of mouth-
     organs and drums,
With ripples like dragon-scales, going grass green
     on the water,
Pleasure lasting, with courtezans, going and coming
     without hindrance,
With the willow flakes falling like snow,
And the vermilioned girls getting drunk about
     sunset,
And the water a hundred feet deep reflecting green
     eyebrows
—Eyebrows painted green are a fine sight in young
     moonlight,
Gracefully painted—
And the girls singing back at each other,
Dancing in transparent brocade,
And the wind lifting the song, and interrupting it,
Tossing it up under the clouds.

        And all this comes to an end.
        And is not again to be met with.
I went up to the court for examination,
Tried Layu's luck, offered the Choyo song,
And got no promotion,
        and went back to the East Mountains
        white-headed.

And once again, later, we met at the South bridge-
      head.

And then the crowd broke up, you went north to
      San palace,

And if you ask how I regret that parting:
      It is like the flowers falling at Spring's end
          Confused, whirled in a tangle.

What is the use of talking, and there is no end of
      talking,

There is no end of things in the heart.

I call in the boy,

Have him sit on his knees here
      To seal this,

And send it a thousand miles, thinking.

By Rihaku.

The Seafarer

(From the early Anglo-Saxon text)

May I for my own self song's truth reckon,
Journey's jargon, how I in harsh days
Hardship endured oft.
Bitter breast-cares have I abided,
Known on my keel many a care's hold,
And dire sea-surge, and there I oft spent
Narrow nightwatch nigh the ship's head
While she tossed close to cliffs. Coldly afflicted,
My feet were by frost benumbed.
Chill its chains are; chafing sighs
Hew my heart round and hunger begot
Mere-weary mood. Lest man know not
That he on dry land loveliest liveth,
List how I, care-wretched, on ice-cold sea,
Weathered the winter, wretched outcast
Deprived of my kinsmen;
Hung with hard ice-flakes, where hail-scur flew,
There I heard naught save the harsh sea
And ice-cold wave, at whiles the swan cries,
Did for my games the gannet's clamour,
Sea-fowl's loudness was for me laughter,
The mews' singing all my mead-drink.

Storms, on the stone-cliffs beaten, fell on the stern
In icy feathers; full oft the eagle screamed
With spray on his pinion.

                    Not any protector
May make merry man faring needy.
This he little believes, who aye in winsome life
Abides 'mid burghers some heavy business,
Wealthy and wine-flushed, how I weary oft
Must bide above brine.
Neareth nightshade, snoweth from north,
Frost froze the land, hail fell on earth then
Corn of the coldest. Nathless there knocketh now
The heart's thought that I on high streams
The salt-wavy tumult traverse alone.
Moaneth alway my mind's lust
That I fare forth, that I afar hence
Seek out a foreign fastness.
For this there's no mood-lofty man over earth's
          midst,
Not though he be given his good, but will have in
          his youth greed;
Nor his deed to the daring, nor his king to the
          faithful

But shall have his sorrow for sea-fare

Whatever his lord will.
He hath not heart for harping, nor in ring-having
Nor winsomeness to wife, nor world's delight
Nor any whit else save the wave's slash,
Yet longing comes upon him to fare forth on the
    water.
Bosque taketh blossom, cometh beauty of berries,
Fields to fairness, land fares brisker,
All this admonisheth man eager of mood,
The heart turns to travel so that he then thinks
On flood-ways to be far departing.
Cuckoo calleth with gloomy crying,
He singeth summerward, bodeth sorrow,
The bitter heart's blood. Burgher knows not—
He the prosperous man—what some perform
Where wandering them widest draweth.
So that but now my heart burst from my breast-
    lock,
My mood 'mid the mere-flood,
Over the whale's acre, would wander wide.
On earth's shelter cometh oft to me,
Eager and ready, the crying lone-flyer,
Whets for the whale-path the heart irresistibly,
O'er tracks of ocean; seeing that anyhow

My lord deems to me this dead life
On loan and on land, I believe not

That any earth-weal eternal standeth
Save there be somewhat calamitous
That, ere a man's tide go, turn it to twain.
Disease or oldness or sword-hate
Beats out the breath from doom-gripped body.
And for this, every earl whatever, for those speak-
      ing after—
Laud of the living, boasteth some last word,
That he will work ere he pass onward,
Frame on the fair earth 'gainst foes his malice,
Daring ado, . . .
So that all men shall honour him after
And his laud beyond them remain 'mid the English,
Aye, for ever, a lasting life's-blast,
Delight mid the doughty.
                    Days little durable,
And all arrogance of earthen riches,
There come now no kings nor Caesars
Nor gold-giving lords like those gone.
Howe'er in mirth most magnified,
Whoe'er lived in life most lordliest,
Drear all this excellence, delights undurable!
Waneth the watch, but the world holdeth.
Tomb hideth trouble. The blade is laid low.

Earthly glory ageth and seareth.

No man at all going the earth's gait,

But age fares against him, his face paleth,

Grey-haired he groaneth, knows gone companions,

Lordly men are to earth o'ergiven,

Nor may he then the flesh-cover, whose life ceaseth,

Nor eat the sweet nor feel the sorry,

Nor stir hand nor think in mid heart,

And though he strew the grave with gold,

His born brothers, their buried bodies

Be an unlikely treasure hoard.

From Rihaku

FOUR POEMS OF DEPARTURE

Light rain is on the light dust.
The willows of the inn-yard
Will be going greener and greener,
But you, Sir, had better take wine ere your departure,
For you will have no friends about you
When you come to the gates of Go.

Separation on the River Kiang

Ko-jin goes west from Ko-kaku-ro,
The smoke-flowers are blurred over the river.
His lone sail blots the far sky.
And now I see only the river,
           The long Kiang, reaching heaven.

Taking Leave of a Friend

Blue mountains to the north of the walls,
White river winding about them;
Here we must make separation
And go out through a thousand miles of dead grass.

Mind like a floating wide cloud.
Sunset like the parting of old acquaintances
Who bow over their clasped hands at a distance.
Our horses neigh to each other
                as we are departing.

Leave-taking near Shoku
"Sanso, King of Shoku, built roads"

THEY say the roads of Sanso are steep,
Sheer as the mountains.
The walls rise in a man's face,
Clouds grow out of the hill
                at his horse's bridle.
Sweet trees are on the paved way of the Shin,
Their trunks burst through the paving,
And freshets are bursting their ice
                in the midst of Shoku, a proud city.

Men's fates are already set,
There is no need of asking diviners.

The City of Choan

THE phoenix are at play on their terrace.
The phoenix are gone, the river flows on alone.
Flowers and grass
Cover over the dark path
           where lay the dynastic house of the Go.
The bright cloths and bright caps of Shin
Are now the base of old hills.

The Three Mountains fall through the far heaven,
The isle of White Heron
           splits the two streams apart.
Now the high clouds cover the sun
And I can not see Choan afar
And I am sad.

South-Folk in Cold Country

THE Dai horse neighs against the bleak wind of
    Etsu,
The birds of Etsu have no love for En, in the north,
Emotion is born out of habit.
Yesterday we went out of the Wild-Goose gate,
To-day from the Dragon-Pen.[1]
Surprised. Desert turmoil. Sea sun.
Flying snow bewilders the barbarian heaven.
Lice swarm like ants over our accoutrements.
Mind and spirit drive on the feathery banners.
Hard fight gets no reward.
Loyalty is hard to explain.
Who will be sorry for General Rishogu,
        the swift moving,
Whose white head is lost for this province?

[1] *I.e.*, we have been warring from one end of the empire to
the other, now east, now west, on each border.

I HAVE not come to the end of Ernest Fenollosa's notes by a long way, nor is it entirely perplexity that causes me to cease from translation. True, I can find little to add to one line out of a certain poem:

> "You know well where it was that I walked
> When you had left me."

In another I find a perfect speech in a literality which will be to many most unacceptable. The couplet is as follows:

> "Drawing sword, cut into water, water again flow:
> Raise cup, quench sorrow, sorrow again sorry."

There are also other poems, notably the "Five colour Screen," in which Professor Fenollosa was, as an art critic, especially interested, and Rihaku's sort of Ars Poetica, which might be given with diffidence to an audience of good will. But if I give them, with the necessary breaks for explanation, and a tedium of notes, it is quite certain that the personal hatred in which I am held by many, and the *invidia* which is directed against me because I have dared openly to declare my belief in certain young artists, will be brought to bear first on the flaws of such translation, and will then be merged into depreciation of the whole book of translations. Therefore I give only these unquestionable poems.

E.P.

NOTES

1   T.S. Eliot, 'Introduction' *Selected Poems* in *Ezra Pound, A Critical Anthology*, ed. J.P. Sullivan (Harmondsworth: Penguin Books, 1970) 105. Hereafter Eliot.

2   Lewis in Humphrey Carpenter, *A Serious Character, The Life of Ezra Pound* (London: Faber and Faber, 1988) 271. Hereafter Carpenter; Sandburg in *Ezra Pound: The Critical Heritage*, ed. Eric Homberger (London: Routledge & Kegan Paul, 1972) 116–17.

3   That same year Giles published *Chinese Without a Teacher: Being a Collection of Easy and Useful Sentences in the Mandarin Dialect.* (London: Kelly & Walsh, 1901).

4   Giles in Zhaoming Qian, *Orientalism and Modernism (The Legacy of China in Pound, and Williams* (Durham: Duke Univ. Press, 1995) 27.

5   Giles in Qian, *Orientalism and Modernism* 28.

6   Pound, *The Spirit of Romance* (1910; New York: New Directions, 1968) 14.

7   Ezra Pound, 'Chinese Written Character', *Early Writings, Poems and Prose*, ed. Ira B. Nadel (New York: Penguin, 2005) 400, 399. Hereafter Early Writings, Nadel.

8   On Pound and Marco Polo, see Dorsey Kleitz, 'Ezra Pound, Marco Polo, and Cathay', *Essays and Studies in British and American Literature* (Tokyo: Tokyo Woman's Christian University) Vol. 50 (2004) 29–43.

9   On the early visions and quests for Cathay, see Arthur Tilley, 'Rabelais and Geographical Discovery', *Modern Language Review* 5 (January 1910) 68–77.

10   Walt Whitman, 'A Broadway Pageant', l.23. Whitman wrote the poem to celebrate the 1860 arrival in New York of Japanese delegates to ratify the US Japan Treaty of Amity and Commerce. It originally appeared in the *New York Times* in June 1860 and then

in *Leaves of Grass*. Selections from Confucius were read at Whitman's funeral.

11   David Weir, *American Orient, Imagining the East from the Colonial Era through the Twentieth Century* (Amherst: Univ. of Massachusetts Press, 2011) 123–4. John Luther Long heard the Butterfly story from his sister who had been living in Tokyo, Yokohama and Nagasaki as the wife of a missionary since 1886. She supposedly heard the story from a peddler. Sanehide Kodama, *American Poetry and Japanese Culture* (Hamden, CT: Archon Books, 1984) 23. Also see Karl E. Meyer and Shareen Blair Brysac, *The China Collectors, America's Century-Long Hunt for Asian Art* (New York: Palgrave Macmillan, 2015).

12   Ralph Waldo Emerson, *Nature* (Boston: James Munroe and Co., 1836) 32.

13   David Weir, *American Orient* 125–6.

14   During the 1840s, Emerson collaborated with Thoreau on the essay 'Ethical Scriptures' where Confucian excerpts appear. And in his journals of 1843–44, Emerson quotes from a translation of *Mencius*. He also read Laurence Oliphant's travel narrative of China of 1860 and Huc's *Travels to China* of 1852. He also read James Legge's translations of Chinese literature to be later studied by Pound.

15   Thoreau, *Walden; or, Life in the Woods*, ed. W. Harding (New York: Houghton Mifflin, 1995) 85; Thoreau, *A Week on the Concord and Merrimack Rivers*, ed. C. Hovde (Princeton: Princeton Univ. Press, 1980) 294. For a fuller discussion of Pound and his transcendental inheritance, see Mark Byron, 'Ezra Pound's Oriental Hinterlands', *Text, Translation, Transnationalism: World Literature in 21st Century Australia*, ed. Peter Morgan. (Sydney: Australian Scholarly Publications, 2015) 1–21.

16   Weir, *American Orient* 124.

17   Moore in Carpenter 266; Ezra Pound to John Quinn in Pound, *The Selected Letters of Ezra Pound to John Quinn, 1915-1924*. Ed. Timothy Materer. (Durham, NC: Duke Univ. Press, 1991) 94.

18   Pound, *Ezra Pound to His Parents, Letters 1895-1929*, ed. Mary de Rachewiltz, A. David Moody, and Joanna Moody (Oxford: Oxford Univ. Press, 2010) 316–7; 318. Hereafter EPP.

19   Pound was also a mover. By December 1911, he had the distinction to be seated at the High Table of the annual Society of Authors dinner at the Criterion Restaurant with Lady and Sir Arthur Conan Doyle and May Sinclair. See Theophilus Boll, *May Sinclair: Novelist*, (Rutherford, NJ: Fairleigh Dickinson Univ. Press, 1973) 95.

20   M.G. Pauthier, *Doctrine de Confucius* (Paris: Librairie Garnier Frères, 1921) ix.

21 Rupert Richard Arrowsmith, *Modernism and the Museum, Asian, African, and Pacific Art and the London Avant-Garde* (Oxford: Oxford Univ. Press, 2011) 109. Hereafter Arrowsmith.

22 Arrowsmith 110.

23 Zhaoming Qian, *Orientalism and Modernism, The Legacy of China in Pound and Williams* (Durham: Duke Univ. Press, 1995) 185 nt.11.

24 Ezra Pound to Dorothy Shakespear, *Ezra Pound and Dorothy Shakespear: Their Letters, 1909-1914*. Ed. Omar Pound and A. Walton Liz (New York: New Directions 1984) 177.

25 Shakespear herself was interested in Chinese painting, a letter from Pound to his father of 3 December 1912 noting that Dorothy is drawing Chinese images. See Zhaoming Qian, *Orientalism and Modernism* (Durham: Duke Univ. Press, 1995), 183 n. 4.

26 Zhaoming Qian, *The Modernist Response to Chinese Art, Pound, Moore, Stevens* (Charlottesville: Univ. Press of Virginia, 2003) 53.

27 Pound in D.G. Bridson, 'An Interview with Ezra Pound,' *New Directions* 17, ed. James Laughlin (New York: New Directions 1959) 177.

28 Zhaoming Qian, *Orientalism and Modernism*, 24; *Ezra Pound and Dorothy Shakespear: Their Letters, 1909-1914*. Ed. Omar Pound and A. Walton Liz (New York: New Directions 1984) 264.

29 Ezra Pound, 'Affirmations,' *Gaudier-Brzeska* (1916; New York: New Directions, 1970) 116–17.

30 *Ezra Pound/ Dorothy Shakespear* 267; Qian, *Orientalism and Modernism* 23–5.

31 Mary Fenollosa, 'Foreword,' *Epochs of Chinese & Japanese Art*, New and revised Ed. with notes by Professor Petrucci, 2nd. Ed. 1913 (New York: Dover Publications, 1963) v–vi. Hereafter *Epochs*.

32 *Epochs* xxx.

33 Qian, *Orientalism and Modernism* 25.

34 Fenollosa in Weir 108.

35 Pound, 'Introduction', *Noh Theatre of Japan with Complete Texts of 15 Classic Plays* (Mineola, New York: Dover Publications,2004) 3. This is a reprint of *Noh or Accomplishment: A Study of the Classical Stage of Japan* originally published in 1917. In a 'Note', Pound says his work has been that of translator 'who has found all the heavy work done for him and who has had but the pleasure of arranging beauty into the words.' He thanks Arthur Waley for corrections for a number of orthographical mistakes in Japanese proper names (p. iv).

36 Karatani in Josephine Nock-Hee Park, *Apparitions of Asia, Modernist Form and Asian American Poetics* (New York: Oxford Univ. Press, 2008) 9.

37 Pound to William Carlos Williams in Pound, *Selected Letters,*

1907-1941, ed. D.D. Paige (1950; New York: New Directions, 1971) 27. Hereafter SL. For a full listing of the first twenty-one folders – there are sixty-two in all – see Zhaoming Qian, *Orientalism and Modernism*, 190–1, ftnt.6. The material, part of the Ezra Pound Papers, is at the Beinecke Rare Book and Manuscript Library, Yale University, New Haven, CT.

38   Pound in SL 27.

39   Carpenter 265–6.

40   Fenollosa in A. David Moody, *Ezra Pound: Poet Vol. I, The Young Genius 1885-1920* (Oxford: Oxford Univ. Press, 2007) 241.

41   F.S. Flint, 'Book of the Week: Recent Verse', *New Age* 722 (11 July 1908) 212.

42   F.S. Flint, 'The History of Imagism', *Egoist* (1 May 1915) 71.

43   Earl Miner, *Japanese Tradition in British and American Literature* (Princeton: Princeton Univ. Press, 1958) 158.

44   Laurence Binyon, *Paintings in the Far East* (London: Edward Arnold, 1908) 6.

45   The four plays are 'Kumasaka', 'Nishikigi', 'Hagoromo' and 'Kagekiyo'.

46   Ezra Pound, 'Introduction', Ernest Fenollosa and Ezra Pound, *The Noh Theatre of Japan* (Mineola, NY: Dover Publications, 2004) 5.

47   EEP 319.

48   Chamberlain in J.B. Harmer, *Victory in Limbo: Imagism 1908-1917* (London: Secker & Warburg, 1975) 128, 133.

49   See David Ewick, themargins.net, an important website for the transcultural dimension of Japanese, Chinese and modernist literature with essential bibliographical information. Ewick offers not only commentary on primary documents but assessments of the reception of Pound's work on Japanese and Chinese writing, citing, for example, T.S. Eliot's 1917 positive response to Pound's Noh for its unity of image, although a year later he declared the work was not so important as *Cathay*.

50   Pound, 'T.S. Eliot', *Literary Essays of Ezra Pound*, ed. T. S. Eliot (New York: New Directions, 1968) 420. The essay originally appeared in *Poetry*, 1917.

51   See Francis A. Johns, 'Manifestations of Arthur Waley: Some Bibliographical and Other Notes,' *British Library Journal* 9.2 (1983) 179.

52   Pound, 'Books Current', *The Future*, II.11 (Nov. 1918) 287. In the same article, Pound reviewed *Oriental Encounters* by M. Pickthall, *Exiles* by James Joyce and *The Sheepfold* by Laurence Housman.

53   For recent praise of Waley's translation, see Ian Buruma, 'The Sensualist', *New Yorker* (20 July 2015) 65–71. Buruma points

out that in ancient Japan, only men wrote in Chinese, a sign of superior status, while women confined themselves to Japanese: 'this explains why the first writers of literary prose in Japanese were highborn women, as were their readers' (66).

54   T.E. Hulme, 'Romanticism and Classicism,' *Speculations*, ed. Herbert Read (New York: Harcourt Brace, 1924) 134–5; Pound, 'Prologomena', *Poetry Review* I.2 (February 1912) 76.

55   See Kern for a discussion of this process and the tradition of translating Chinese into English. Kern also highlights the impact of *Cathay* on *The Cantos*. Robert Kern, *Orientalism, Modernism, and the American Poem* (Cambridge: Cambridge Univ. Press, 1996) 155 ff. Hereafter Kern.

56   Pound in *Early Writings*, Nadel 210.

57   In Carpenter 265.

58   In Carpenter 265.

59   Pound in SL 101. In her review, Buss notes that Pound once wrote to her 'that life was too complicated to be treated coherently in hurried writing'. One might say that about his poems, she adds: 'They are too complicated for hasty judgment'. Furthermore, 'he has an individual fashion of saying things and he is without fear'. Buss, 'Ezra Pound: Some Evidence of his Rare Chinese Quality', *Ezra Pound: The Critical Heritage*, ed. Eric Homberger (London: Routledge, 1972) 125.

60   Pound in *Early Writings*, Nadel 86–8.

61   Eliot 106.

62   Eliot 106.

63   EPP 336, 338.

64   See Appendix: *Cathay, The Text* 113 . Hereafter *Cathay.*

65   Wai-lim Yip, *Ezra Pound's Cathay* (Princeton: Princeton UP, 1969) 88. Hereafter Yip.

66   Pound in Hugh Kenner, *The Pound Era* (Berkeley: Univ. of California Press, 1971) 150.

67   Yip 84.

68   See *Ezra Pound, The Critical Heritage*, ed. Eric Homberger (London: Routledge & Kegan Paul, 1972) 118, 111.

69   In Carpenter 271.

70   *The Bookman*, 48 (July 1915) 112 in Nelson, *Elkin Mathews* 277: ftn 66.

71   See for example Achilles Fang, 'Fenollosa and Pound', *Harvard Journal of Asian Studies* XX (1957) 213–38, or Arthur Waley who remarked that 'Exile's Letter' is at best a 'brilliant paraphrase' in Waley, *The Poetry and Career of Li Po* (London: 1950) 11. Also see Wai-lim Yip, *Ezra Pound's Cathay* (Princeton: Princeton UP,

1969) and his comparison of a literal translation of 'The Lament of the Frontier Guard' with Fenollosa's 'crippled text' and Pound's imaginative treatment, 84–88.

72   Eliot, xvi.

73   George Steiner, *After Babel, Aspects of Language and Translation* (London: Oxford Univ. Press, 1975) 358. Hereafter Steiner.

74   'Chinese Poetry II' in *Early Writings*, Nadel 302.

75   'Chinese Written Character' in *Early Writings*, Nadel 306.

76   W.B. Yeats, 'Introduction', *Oxford Book of Modern Verse 1892–1935* (Oxford: Oxford Univ. Press, 1936) xl.

77   See Arrowsmith, *Modernism and the Museum* 159.

78   A. David Moody, in the first volume of his biography of Pound, outlines these themes plus parallels between the Emperor of Rihaku's world and the government and King of Britain during the First World War. For Moody, the social and political implications of the text dominate. See A. David Moody, *Ezra Pound: Poet, Vol. I, The Young Genius 1885–1920* (Oxford: Oxford Univ. Press, 2007) 270–2.

79   *Cathay* 85.

80   In 1920 in a note to his collection *Umbra*, Pound described 'The Seafarer', as well as 'Exile's Letter', and *Cathay* in general as 'major personae'.

81   The poems are 'Sennin Poem by Kakuhaku', 'A Ballad of the Mulberry Road', 'Old Idea of Choan by Rosoriu' and 'To-Em-Mei's "The Unmoving Cloud"'.

82   'Chinese Writing in' *Early Writings*, Nadel 297.

83   *Cathay* 113.

84   *Cathay* 88.

85   See Mark Byron's discussion in 'Ezra Pound's "Seven Lakes Canto": Poetry and Painting, From East to West,' *Rikkyo Review: Arts and Letters* 73 (2013) 121–42.

86   Kern 194.

87   *Cathay* 86.

88   *Cathay* 92–93.

89   *Cathay* 103.

90   Ronald Bush, 'Pound and Li Po: *What Becomes a Man*', *Ezra Pound Among the Poets*, ed. George Bornstein (Chicago: Univ. of Chicago Press, 1985), 36–7, 60–1.

91   William Tay, *Literary Relations* (Taipei: Dongda tushu, 1987) 176. For a summary of reactions, also see Yip.

92   Mathews had an interest in the Far East as it was then called and published the work of his friend the Japanese poet Yoni Noguchi. His elegantly printed multi-volume *The Pilgrimage: A Book of*

Poems, beginning with *From the Eastern Sea*, printed on Japanese paper with a frontispiece after Utamaro and bound, as Mathews advertised, 'in Japanese style', appeared between 1910 and 1915. In 1910, Mathews also published Noguchi's *Lafcadio Hearn in Japan* which went into a second edition in 1911. *The American Diary of a Japanese Girl* by Noguchi appeared in 1912 and *Through the Torii* in 1914. Pound knew of the volumes and naturally thought Mathews, who published his previous work, would be interested in *Cathay*. He was.

For these and other publishing details, see James G. Nelson, *Elkin Mathews, Publisher to Yeats, Joyce, Pound* (Madison: Univ. of Wisconsin Press, 1989) 152–3.

93   *Cathay* 97.

94   'Introduction to Taoist Poetry', http://personaltao.com/gallery/poetry/.

95   Fletcher, 'The Orient and Contemporary Poetry', *The Asian Legacy and American Life*, ed. Arthur E. Christy (New York: Asia Press, 1945) 146; Ewick, John Gould Fletcher, http://themargins.net/bib/B/BH/bh15.html.

96   *Cathay* 92.

97   Kenneth Rexroth, *World Outside the Window: Selected Essays of Kenneth Rexroth*, ed. Bradford Morrow (New York: New Directions 1987) 187.

98   *Cathay* 95.

99   Kern 193.

100   *Early Writings*, Nadel 253.

101   Kern 193.

102   *Cathay* 113.

103   Pound, 'Terminal Note', *The Chinese Written Character as a Medium of Poetry* (London: Stanley Nott, 1936) 33; Pound, *The Spirit of Romance* (1910; New York: New Directions,1968) 222.

104   *Early Writings*, Nadel 298–303.

105   *Cathay* 94.

FURTHER READING

Bush, Christopher, *Ideographic Modernism: China, Writing, Media*. New York: Oxford Univ. Press, 2010.

Chapple, Anne S. 'Ezra Pound's *Cathay*: Compilation from the Fenollosa Notebooks,' *Paideuma* 17.2–3 (1988) 9–46.

De Gruchy, John. *Orienting Arthur Waley: Japonism, Orientalism, and the Creation of Japanese Literature in English*. Honolulu: Univ. of Hawaii Press, 2003.

Egan, Jim. *Oriental Shadows: The Presence of the East in Early American Literature*. Columbus, Ohio: Ohio State Univ. Press, 2011.

Hakutani, Yoshinobu. *Haiku and Modernist Poetics*. New York: Palgrave Macmillan, 2009.

Harmer, J.B. *Victory in Limbo: Imagism 1908–1917*. London: Secker & Warburg, 1975.

Kodama, Sanehide. *American Poetry and Japanese Culture*. Hamden, CT: Archon Books, 1984.

Moody, A. David. *Ezra Pound: Poet, Vol. I, The Young Genius 1885-1920*. Oxford: Oxford Univ. Press, 2007.

Qian, Zhaoming, ed. *Ezra Pound's Chinese Friends, Stories in Letters*. New York: Oxford Univ. Press, 2008.

Qian, Zhaoming, ed. *Ezra Pound in China*. Ann Arbor: Univ. of Michigan Press, 2003.

Qian, Zhaoming, ed. *Modernism and the Orient*. New Orleans: Univ. of New Orleans Press, 2012.

Steiner, George. *After Babel: Aspects of Language and Translation*. London: Oxford Univ. Press, 1975.

Waley, Arthur. *The Nō Plays of Japan*. With Letters by Oswald Sickert. 1920. New York: Grove Press, 1957.

Xie, Ming. *Ezra Pound and the Appropriation of Chinese Poetry, Cathay, Translation and Imagism*. New York: Garland, 1999.

ACKNOWLEDGEMENTS

My thanks to Imogen Liu at Penguin China for suggesting this short study. David Ewick of Tokyo Woman's Christian University has been an invaluable friend and source of all things Asian for Pound. His fingertip knowledge of Oriental modernism and its sources is unsurpassed and his website themargins.net, founded in 2003, is the reliable centre for matters relating to Japan, the Orient and English-language writers. The site divides into an archive of Japan in English-language verse and 'Japonisme, Orientalism, Modernism, a Bibliography of Japan in English-Language Verse of the Early 20th Century'.

Other Poundians who have contributed directly and indirectly include Zhaoming Qian, A.D. Moody, Ron Bush, Demetres Tryphonopolous, Kent Su and the late Patricia Cockram, Daniel Albright, Burton Hatlen and James Laughlin. Special thanks to Mary de Rachewiltz for unfolding the eighteenth century screen book owned by Pound and his parents. Special thanks, as well, to Mark Byron and Dorsey Kleitz for sharing their research on Pound and American Orientalism and Pound and Marco Polo with me. And as always, deep love to Dara, Ryan and Anne for their support, laughter and patience.

Radish

MO YAN

'That dark-skinned boy with the superhuman ability to suffer and a superhuman degree of sensitivity represents the soul of my entire fictional output.' – Mo Yan

During China's collectivist era in the late 1950s, a rural work team responsible for building an important floodgate receives a strange new recruit: Hei-hai, a skinny, silent and almost feral boy. Assigned to assist the blacksmith at the worksite forge, Hei-hai proves superhumanly indifferent to pain and suffering and yet, eerily sensitive to the natural world. As the worksite succumbs to jealousy and strife, Hei-hai's eyes remain fixed on a world that only he can see, searching for wonders that only he understands. One day, he finds all that he has been seeking embodied in the most mundane and unexpected way: a radish.

Mo Yan (literally 'don't speak') is the pen name of Guan Moye. Born in 1955 to a peasant family in Shandong province, he is the author of ten novels including Frog and Red Sorghum, dozens of novellas and hundreds of short stories. He is the winner of the 2012 Nobel Prize in Literature and the 2009 Newman Prize for Chinese Literature.

'Pungent, potent, absurd, moving, and alive, this early Mo Yan novella carries his unmistakable stamp. Survival is ignoble, and power blunt, but glimpses of the transcendent are possible: Radish captures the human condition with aching force.' Gish Jen, author of Mona in the Promised Land

www.penguin.com.cn

PENGUIN
SPECIALS

Beethoven in China

JINDONG CAI AND SHEILA MELVIN

How the great composer became an icon in the People's Republic

At the turn of the twentieth century, students returning from abroad introduced Beethoven to China. The composer's perseverance in the face of adversity and his musical genius resonated in a nation searching for a way forward. Beethoven remained a durable part of Chinese life in the decades that followed, becoming an icon to intellectuals, music fans and party cadres alike, playing a role in major historical events from the May Fourth Movement to the normalisation of US-China relations. Jindong Cai, whose love for the musician began during the Cultural Revolution, and culture journalist Sheila Melvin tell the compelling story of Beethoven and the Chinese people.

Jindong Cai is an orchestra conductor and a professor at Stanford University. He is a three-time recipient of the American Society of Composers, Authors and Publishers award for Adventurous Programming of Contemporary Music.

Sheila Melvin has been writing about culture in China for over 20 years. She is the author of *Rhapsody in Red* (co-authored with Jindong) and *The Little Red Book of China Business*.